THE SUBURBAN
FARMER'S HANDBOOK

The Suburban Farmer's Handbook

A COMPREHENSIVE GUIDE
TO GROWING AND PRESERVING
YOUR OWN FOOD AND DRINK

by Jack Kramer

Drawings by Robert Johnson

Photographs by Waldo Bascom

DOUBLEDAY & COMPANY, INC., GARDEN CITY, NEW YORK
1977

Library of Congress Cataloging in Publication Data
Kramer, Jack, 1927–
The suburban farmer's handbook.
Includes index.
1. Vegetable gardening. 2. Fruit-culture.
3. Nuts. 4. Food—Preservation. I. Title.
SB321.K72   635
ISBN 0-385-11008-1
Library of Congress Catalog Card Number 76-2789

Contents

Contents

THE SUBURBAN
FARMER'S HANDBOOK

1.

The Land: Suburban and City Gardens

Growing your own food can be pleasurable as well as profitable. Growing plants provides more than solace for the soul; it also supplies food for the table. But just what you can and cannot grow on your particular land deserves consideration. Total self-sufficiency with cows, horses, goats, chickens, and pigs takes as much as five acres of land. Frankly, for the average family a small vegetable garden, a few berry bushes, and some fruit trees are usually all that can be managed on a small piece of land.

If vegetables or fruit trees seem like too much trouble, or you do not have the time, you might just want to forage elsewhere for wild plants and enjoy their healthful benefits, or perhaps make a little homemade wine for fun and profit. A small herb garden or a more extensive one (you need a plot only 5×5 feet) can yield much bounty if you are into herbal teas and brews and want fresh herbs for cooking.

One year you can devote the land to vegetables, the next year you can grow some herbs; just alternate schedules as it suits your preference. If you want to keep the summer garden through the winter, try canning and drying food. If you have a small greenhouse (and this can be an inexpensive, homemade one), you can grow more things to help cut food costs. If space is very limited outdoors, you can grow sprouts indoors, put midget vegetables on the window sill, and on and on. Thus, there are all sorts of directions your gardening tastes can go in, both indoors and out.

Do not try to do too much on too little. It is much better to have a good, small vegetable garden and a small orchard than too many plants on too little land where nothing will grow properly. I garden on about one acre of land and am able to supply many of my own vegetables most of the year, fruit in season (from trees on the property), and some berries and nuts. I also grow annuals and perennials for cut flowers. This harvest also gives me some security against high food prices.

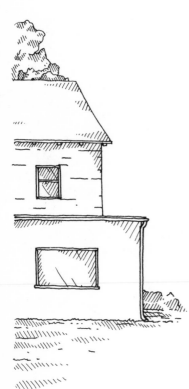

Just what you do and what you grow in your garden will be governed by the growing space you have. City people are of course more restricted in what rewards they can coax from nature because in town space is limited—a balcony, window box, rooftop, or porch. Suburban gardeners have more latitude and can enjoy more garden activities and bounty.

To succeed you must work within your limitation. City people who want their own honey are dreaming because bees are not apartment dwellers. Nor can city people have their own wine since growing grapes in the living room just does not work. But there are many other crops that can grow quite well under city conditions.

THE SMALL SITE

The typical half-acre site found in many suburban communities offers varied possibilities for plants. Consider a 50×100-foot plot. Here there is space for both ornamental and food gardens. With proper planning and planting you can feed your family vegetables almost all year. You can also grow some fruit trees and herbs and have your bees too if you know what you are doing. The small or average site can provide a treasure house of good savings, and the vegetable patch comes first.

You can grow dozens of vegetables (for specifics see Chapter 5), but again, do not tackle too much. Plan on some greens for salads. Grow root crops like beets and carrots. Radishes will practically grow by themselves. Have peas and squash, beans and tomatoes and save a great deal of money. Vegetable gardening will of course cost you some money too—and time. You will need soil and fertilizers, plants (prestarted) or seeds.

On a small site a few fruit trees are certainly within reason, and once established, apples and peaches, pears and cherries will care for themselves. The initial cost will be reasonable—with fruit trees it is more a question of how much time you can give them. Some pruning and spraying are necessary.

Many people who grow vegetables and fruits often forget about a cutting garden, but they shouldn't. Having fresh flowers in the home is a joy, and florist flowers, beautiful as they are, are costly. Cut flowers you grow yourself are very reasonable.

A few nut trees and some berries will round out the average small "farm."

If your property is more extensive, then there is certainly room for having apiaries or growing grapes. Again, just what you grow will depend on how much land you have and how you parcel it; the following

chapters will discuss all kinds of fruits, berries and vegetables for you to try.

THE CITY GARDENER

The city gardener may have only a small yard, a rooftop area, or a porch that can be converted into a place for plants. Generally, I feel, the city gardener should opt for an ornamental garden that is beautiful to look at rather than a garden for eating, but with intelligent planning the city farmer can also actually grow a bit of produce.

A small vegetable garden is well within reason—you can vertically grow vining vegetables like squash and beans on trellises, or even tomatoes, to save space. Herbs are very desirable for the city garden and grow well, and a few choice annuals and perennials can be tucked in here and there to beautify the scene and add color to the property.

Container Gardening

If you are a city gardener, you may have to rely heavily on container gardening.

Gardening in boxes and tubs is a fine way to have plants if you do not have any property or if soil is bad. This method of gardening also gives you the latitude of moving plants around if they do not prosper in one area. You can grow almost any plant you want in containers, from trees to shrubs to flowers and vegetables. But do not garden in just any container. For the best results and looks, make your own planters: A modular container garden with well-made planters looks 200 per cent better than a few purchased tubs and pots stuck here and there outside. (And today's incredibly high costs of purchased containers makes building your own boxes and tubs an economical plus.) Modular gardens are simply boxes of the same size; the boxes can be used interchangeably throughout the garden area, stacked, tiered, or along walls, or whatever—there are dozens of arrangements.

Use redwood for your containers because it is a natural, rot-resistant wood and lasts at least two to four years, even without preservatives. You can make boxes from 1-inch stock, but 2-inch stock is much better and lasts longer. Use construction-grade redwood; kiln-dried or finished lumber is not necessary and is just too expensive.

Douglas fir is more expensive than redwood and needs a preservative coating, but it is a strong wood. Pine can also be used, but it is soft, deteriorates in weather faster than other woods, and needs a preservative (sold at hardware stores).

You can nail boxes together, but they will last longer if you use brass screws and high-quality wood epoxies.

Growing plants in containers requires somewhat different cultural rules than growing directly in the ground. Plants in boxes or tubs require more water and more feeding. Be sure soil is evenly moist and do fertilize plants with a general plant food such as 10-10-5 in spring once they are growing well. Use the plant food twice a month through the warm season.

Remember that plants in large tubs or boxes will not need as much water as, say, plants in small containers (up to 8 or 10 inches). Large containers of soil hold water longer than small ones. In general, you will find container growing a successful venture, especially if you live in areas where soil is sandy or claylike. Container gardening gives you the opportunity to furnish proper soil for maximum plant growth, and do use the best soil you can get—one that is full of nutrients and has good porosity.

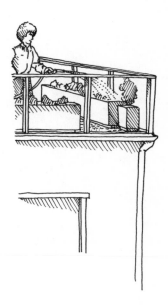

ROOFTOP/PORCH GARDENS

These gardens can occupy any porch or roof that can support the weight. Say you have a two-story home with one flat roof. This tar and gravel space can be easily converted to a garden, no matter how small it is. A garage roof is a perfect place for a food garden. A second-floor greenhouse is another possibility if there is one small room of the upper story that is rarely used as a room. Take off the roof, install glass (or leave it open), and make your garden part of the house.

There are innumerable places (once you start to look) with a level roof or porch where you can enjoy gardening. One of the finest garage rooftop gardens I ever saw was in Chicago, where peppers and tomatoes flourished in the heat of summer. And in my Chicago apartment the floor of the back porch was wooden, with railings, and about 8×20 feet. The porch had a brick wall that was perfect for hanging pot plants. Along the railings I installed planter beds with annuals, perennials, and so forth; I even raised vegetables.

If you want a rooftop or porch garden, do not worry about exposures because there are plants for all areas; what you eventually have depends on the available space and roof supports, barriers, overhead screens and canopies, containers, and so on. You can grow vegetables and herbs in boxes, have annuals and perennials, and even trees and shrubs can be grown to add beauty to the garden in the air. Follow container growing aids suggested earlier for your rooftop greeneries.

THE APARTMENT DWELLER

The person who lives in an apartment and badly needs some greenery usually relegates what space there

[6]

is to house plants, which is fine. But lately even the ur-
banite has started to grow some tomatoes or a few
other vegetables at window sills or in window boxes.
The apartment dweller cannot grow everything, but
there are some plants that make sense for indoor resi-
dents. Tomatoes are the first choice, and many midget
varieties have been developed for apartment growing.
Small eggplants have worked well for friends of mine,
and hanging baskets of lettuce are very satisfactory.
Herb gardens are well within the realm of the apartment dweller, and growing sprouts (which can be
picked in a few days) are immensely popular.

There are many pleasures and profits from food gardening with all kinds of plants for all kinds of gardeners. Pick and choose, pluck what is good, discard
the rest. Make your choice fit your situation and then
go and grow.

2.

Greenhouse Dividends

Whether you have a homemade greenhouse or a prefab unit, a greenhouse can add much pleasure and profit to your gardening year. A greenhouse is a place to start plants, to grow seeds, to store bulbs over winter, and so on—a veritable treasure house of garden things to do to save money and time (plants too).

Conditions in a greenhouse are ideal for most plants, and you can of course grow vegetables in summer, have herbs, or just use the greenhouse as a refreshing place for ailing house plants. (This alone would save money and give you the satisfaction of nursing sick plants back to health.)

Let us explore a little of the greenhouse know-how so you will know how to get the most from your garden under glass.

FOR PLEASURE

The greenhouse offers many avenues of gardening pleasure. For example, a garden under glass filled with tropical plants in winter when it is gray and snowy outside is a psychological lift for anyone. And if you have had trouble growing plants at windows (not enough humidity or air circulation), in a greenhouse your house plants will thrive.

You can grow many plants in your greenhouse that it would be impossible to grow in the home, such as exotic beauties like papayas and guavas or Venus's-flytraps and other insectivorous plants. You can collect only one group of plants such as begonias or orchids (some of these plants grow indoors but not all of them).

In your greenhouse you will be able to putter and work with nature close at hand. This also provides mild but good exercise and when you close your greenhouse door you shut out the busy world so the garden under glass can also be a retreat.

FOR PROFIT

We discuss growing plants from seed in Chapter 4 and the greenhouse is an ideal place to start seeds because conditions are better than in the normal home. You can grow your own house plants (and save acres of money) or start vegetables for outdoor use later or leave them to bear in the greenhouse; many vegetables such as lettuce and tomatoes, squash and eggplant can be easy greenhouse crops for you.

You can have cut flowers. Carnations and chrysanthemums, snapdragons and calendulas are all possibilities for greenhouse growing. You can start these plants in greenhouse benches or in "flats" (shallow wooden boxes) or in standard clay pots.

You can also grow annuals and perennials for your

outdoor use and profit greatly. Prestarted nursery plants cost money but seeds you start are economical. Start the seeds as described in Chapter 4. You can grow: ageratum, antirrhinum, calendula, centaurea, cosmos, gaillardia, impatiens, lobelia, petunia, salpiplossis, tagetes.

Vegetables are a fabulous bounty for greenhouse growing and tomatoes, carrots, and radishes—lettuce too—can certainly be grown under glass and with good results. Use large tubs for tomatoes, hanging baskets for lettuce, for example. Keep them in the greenhouse or start them there to transfer to the garden when the weather is settled. Herbs too can be part of the glass garden and a few selected ones such as basil and dill, tarragon and chives are always welcome crops.

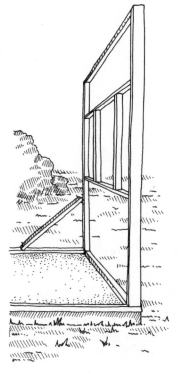

Over the winter you can store bulbous plants such as vallotas, cyclamens, gloxinias, and such that need a dry rest for several months. Simply leave bulbs in pots and store under benches. Then you can start them again the following year rather than having to buy new plants.

You can grow mushrooms and endive in the greenhouse and even use the greenhouse as a storage place for canned or preserved foods. This means modifying the temperature somewhat and shuttering the greenhouse but it can be done. In this case the greenhouse is used like the old-fashioned root cellars.

There are indeed innumerable ways to make the greenhouse a place of pleasure and profit as well. Even the most crude homemade greenhouse offers all these advantages and you need not spend a fortune in making a greenhouse. (For information on building your own plant place see my book *Your Homemade Greenhouse and How to Build It*.)

GREENHOUSE CONDITIONS

Once you have built your greenhouse, you must consider such requirements as temperature, humidity, and ventilation. If the greenhouse is an all-glass, tightly enclosed room, these requirements are vital because glass is a poor conductor and greenhouses are invariably too hot in summer and too cold in winter. However, if you have avoided the all-glass unit, the problems of temperature, humidity, and ventilation are less stringent. Basically, conditions that approximate home conditions, that is, average temperatures of 70° to 80° F. during the day and some cooling at night, are fine. Humidity of 30 to 60 per cent is ideal, along with year-round circulation of air, which plants need.

HUMIDITY

There is no reason to be confused about humidity in relation to growing plants. Average humidity (30 to 50 per cent) is fine for most plants. High humidity, which is often recommended for plants, can do more harm than good in the winter because when coupled with dark days it can create a breeding ground for plant fungus and bacteria. Use an inexpensive hygrometer in the greenhouse to measure the moisture in the air. And remember that the more artificial heat you use in winter, the more moisture in the air will be necessary. On very hot days keep the humidity somewhat high. At night, humidity, like temperature, should be lower if you want good plant growth.

Usually, many plants growing together will create their own humidity, so expensive equipment (misters, foggers) is not necessary unless it is very hot. As long as you water routinely, there will be sufficient humidity in a room of plants to create good growth.

TEMPERATURE

Most plants do just fine with a temperature of 70° to 80° F. during the day and a ten- to fifteen-degree drop at night. You can maintain this temperature range in your own greenhouse without elaborate equipment; only in winter will you need to adjust heat for those very cold nights (and a few very cold nights will not harm plants). What will harm plants are sudden changes in temperatures, but by opening windows and doors you can cool summer temperatures somewhat. On very hot days, even the home greenhouse of wood and glass can get too hot for plants. Even with doors and windows open, the sun can push the inside temperature past 100° F., which desiccates plants and causes them to lose moisture too fast. Spray and mist plants with water to keep them cool. Be especially alert in prolonged heat spells because you can lose many plants in a short few days if you do not cool them by misting or by providing outside shade.

In winter, do not fret if the greenhouse is somewhat cool. It is far better to keep plants cool than too hot; they can recover from a chill but rarely from dehydration. However, on very windy and cold days, the temperature in a greenhouse can drop faster than you think, so make sure sufficient heat is provided. Again, avoid drastic temperature changes in the greenhouse.

VENTILATION

I have always considered ventilation in my greenhouse more important than humidity or temperature because a good circulation of air is essential for all plants. Good ventilation provides relief from the sun, helps control such disease problems as mildew, and assures good humidity. The atmosphere in the greenhouse should be buoyant and fresh, never stagnant or stale. If you observe nature, you will note that few plants grow in stagnant places. Take a clue from Mother Nature: Keep ventilation at a maximum in your greenhouse. And even in winter be sure some air is entering the greenhouse. Remember that hot air rises, so provide some window facilities at the top of the greenhouse. When windows or vents are open, warm air flows out to cool the greenhouse and provides fresh air for best growing conditions.

SHADING

Direct summer sun can heat up a greenhouse considerably and wreak havoc on plants. For example, some might die overnight if subject to even one day of extreme heat above 100° F., and leaf temperatures over 120° F. immediately scorch and kill plant cells. In most parts of the country, unless your greenhouse is at an east exposure (getting only morning sun), you are going to have to provide some shading for the structure.

Old-fashioned paste or whiting powder can be applied with a spray or paintbrush, but this is a bother and ugly-looking. Instead, use movable aluminum- or wood-slatted Venetian blinds or bamboo roll-ups. They cost more than powders or paints, but they look better, are easy to install, and can be opened during periods of only bright light.

Plastic shading, like paint or powder, is also a bother and looks terrible. Use some nice curtains that break the sunlight yet allow some light through. Even better is special window treillage, which adds great charm to a building. (This is my preference, after trying other methods of shading.) Trellises can be built cheaply and installed with little effort; they will provide almost perfect light for plants as alternating shade and light are created.

HEATING

Heating the greenhouse depends mainly on where you live, the size of the greenhouse, and the design.

Once greenhouse heating was a maze of pipes and problems, and only hot-water heat was considered for plants. Today we know that many other types of heating are suitable. Installation and operation of the heating unit are not too difficult, but determining what kind of heating fuel to use—gas, oil, or electricity—can be tricky.

Before you select the heating system for your greenhouse, check local gas and electric rates. Decide which will be the most economical and then investigate specific systems. For my small greenhouse I used forced hot-air heat by extending one duct from the house furnace. A professional installed the duct for $60. A small furnace with about three ducts (for the average greenhouse) would cost no more than $400.

The warm-air-gas-fired heater is popular for greenhouses; it has a safety pilot and thermostatic controls. You may have to provide masonry or metal chimneys so fumes are released outside. A non-vented heater does not need an outlet chimney; the combustible chamber is sealed and outside the greenhouse. The heater extends about 10 inches inside the greenhouse and needs only a 17×20-inch wall opening. Both types of heaters are approved by the American Gas Association (AGA) and are available through greenhouse dealers.

The warm-air-oil-fired heater is small, able to fit under a greenhouse bench. It will furnish sufficient heat for most average-sized greenhouses. It has a gun-type burner, a blower, a two-stage fuel pump, and full controls. The heater requires a masonry chimney or a metal smokestack above the roof.

Electric heaters are also satisfactory for small greenhouses. These units are automatic, built with a circulating fan, but heavy-duty electrical lines are necessary. The heater and thermostats should be installed by a professional in accordance with local electric codes.

3.

Knowing the Basics

No matter how much, or how little, land you have, you will need to know how to grow plants properly to get the most out of it. To be a good gardener you should know something about soil, and how plants grow. Then you can get the most from your land no matter what its size.

SOIL

Generally we do not think about soil; it is merely "dirt" under our feet or something to be used as a site for a building foundation. But for a producing garden, soil is of the utmost importance. It cannot be just any earth; it must be soil that contains enough nutrients to support plant life.

In nature, as the seasons change, so does the soil—it is replenished naturally by the environmental cycle of decay and death. However, the soil in your garden exists under a totally different set of "rules." The land has been cleared prior to the building of the house, so most likely good topsoil has been stripped by the bulldozer. The trees and shrubs that once furnished natural vegetation (falling leaves create humus, which is high organic matter) have been removed to make room for your house and site. What is left on most properties is either sandy, clayey, or spent soil, which requires cultivation and replenishing if plants are to grow. This involves turning the soil and breaking it up so it is porous, and adding compost or humus to it. If your soil is sandy, water will run right through it and plants will not absorb moisture. In a clayey soil, water cannot penetrate to plant roots.

A good soil is friable (crumbly) and has porosity (small air spaces in it). Soil must have humus; humus improves the water-holding capacity of any topsoil and has the physical ability to hold and distribute moisture evenly. Without air circulating through the soil, there would be no life within the soil. A friable soil ensures a good circulation of necessary gases in the soil. Oxygen is absolutely needed by roots below ground if plants are to prosper. The vital inert gas nitrogen also enters soils through air passages and is transformed into usable plant food.

It is also important to know just what kind of soil you have because some plants prefer acidic conditions, others alkaline. The pH scale measures the acidity or alkalinity of soil. You can determine the pH of the soil by testing it with the kits advertised in garden magazines or you can have it tested by the state agricultural authorities.

Soil with a pH of 7 is neutral; below 7 the soil is acidic and above 7 it is alkaline. Most plants like a neutral soil which registers 7 on the pH scale. Some, as

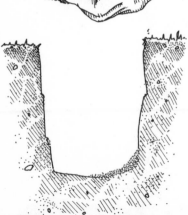

previously mentioned, grow better in an acidic soil and several types prefer an alkaline soil.

To lower the pH of soil (increase the acidity), apply ground sulfur at the rate of 1 pound to 100 square feet. Spread the sulfur on top of the soil and apply water; this lowers the pH symbol about one point. To raise the pH of soil (sweeten it) add ground limestone at the rate of 10 pounds per 150 square feet. Scatter the limestone on the soil and water. It is best to add ground limestone in several applications at four- or six-week intervals instead of using a lot of it at one time.

Water, the lifeline of a garden, depends almost entirely on the structure of the soil to perform its proper function. Water transforms elements into usable plant food. When plant food minerals are free, they are dissolved or suspended in water; then the plants can draw up this water.

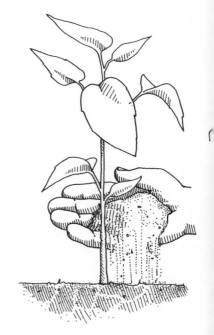

COMPOSTING

Compost has been widely publicized in the last few years, and its importance as a vital element of a good garden soil is now fully realized. However, making the compost is not that fully understood. Just any old pile of garbage is not going to do the job, and compost making is not the joy some writers make it appear—it is hard work, and usually smelly! You can now buy compost in tidy packages, but the cost for any appreciable amount is liable to leave you bankrupt, so let us consider why your soil needs compost, what compost is, and how to make compost.

To understand the value of compost, just look at the forest floor: There is a build-up of decayed leaves and other natural, organic materials—mushrooms, animal dung, earthworms, and microbes. This supply of humus is replenished yearly. But your garden does not replenish humus, so you must supply humus to the soil as trees

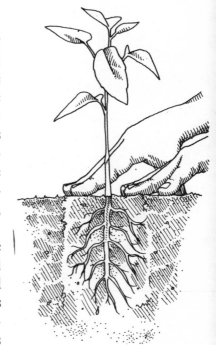

and plants use it up. The process of making the humus is called composting.

Before you plan on what materials to use for compost, first build a wooden or wire compost bin. Do not waste money on commercially made compost bins. Simply install four wooden posts in each corner of an out-of-sight area, say, 5×10 feet, and nail on 2×12-foot rough redwood boards. Even easier is to nail close-mesh wire fencing to the four posts. Leave an opening at one end of the bin to get compost in and out.

You can use any organic matter for the compost: raked leaves, twigs, trimming, cuttings—any surplus green matter and some animal manure (available in tidy packages at nurseries). Put the green clippings into the bin first, and then add a thin layer of manure. The manure provides the extra nitrogen bacteria and fungi need as food; the bacteria and fungi will break down the organic matter. Now add a thin layer of soil, to hold in heat. Next, add a sprinkling of lime, and as the pile decomposes, add some nitrogen granules, which will cause the trash to decay further. Finally, add some pulverized steer manure (in packages) or cottonseed meal.

Generally, you will not have to add activators or starters to the compost mix if you follow the above suggestions because there should be enough bacteria, and the extra nitrogen added will get things going.

Turn the pile occasionally by digging; move the bottom material to the top and repeat the process every few weeks. You should have usable compost in a few months.

Air as well as moisture is necessary in the compost heap, so drive a few stakes into the pile and then remove them, leaving air tubes. Sprinkle the heap occasionally to keep it moist, but never wet; if the heap is too wet, air will not penetrate the heap. If it rains frequently, rig up some type of cover—a tarp or board—over the bin to keep water from soaking the compost.

MULCHING

An easy garden practice that is often ignored is mulching. Mulching decreases the amount of moisture lost through evaporation from soil surfaces and keeps the soil cooler than when it is fully exposed to the sun. Mulching also helps control weed development: Under a protective coating, many weeds fail to germinate, or if they do, they are weak and easy to remove.

Generally, mulches are organic materials that decay in time, contributing to soil improvement. Spread a mulch between plants and around each plant, covering the soil. Apply the mulch in a layer 2 to 4 inches thick around the crown of the plant. Remember that no one mulch does everything. For example, some mulches allow more air to enter the soil than others. Oak leaves and pine needles have an acid content, which is a vital requirement for azaleas, rhododendrons, and other acid-preference plants. So use appropriate mulches in different places around your garden.

Some growers keep plants mulched all year, whereas others apply a mulch after the soil has warmed up in spring and growth has started. If mulches are put in place too early, they stop growth because soil stays cool. For winter protection, apply mulches after the soil has frozen.

Organic Mulches

Leaves. Old leaves are best; oak leaves and pine needles are just right for acid-loving plants.

Hay and straw. Salt hay is best because it decomposes slowly and is weed-free.

Grass clippings. Good when mixed with a coarse material so they do not mat.

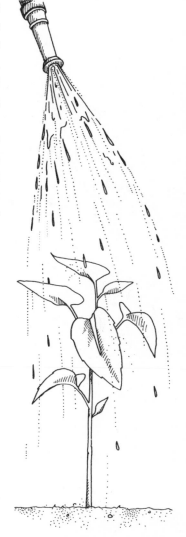

[*21*]

Cocoa beans and pecan shells. Decompose slowly and make a satisfactory mulch, but do not use for acid-loving plants.

Ground fir bark. Several grades; extremely good material that decomposes slowly, is attractive, and stays in place.

Sawdust. Usually free for the asking and quite satisfactory as a mulch. Use it alone, or mix it with peat.

Conifer boughs. Used for winter mulching for flowers and shrubs. Give protection against snow and sun.

There are also inorganic mulches such as stones and gravel, roofing paper, black plastic sheet, or insulated fiber, but of course these materials will not help improve the soil.

HOW PLANTS GROW

Plant growth is determined by light, temperature, and water, as well as kind of soil and nutrients in the soil. Rarely is there a precise balance of all elements, so the gardener must help to modify the temperature for the plants, provide shade if necessary, and apply moisture when it is needed.

A plant, like a pet, becomes a responsibility and requires care. Some plants get along fine with little care; others need more attention; and mature plants, like mature pets, get along with less fuss than young ones.

Vegetables have to be grown quickly, almost nonstop, and need buckets of water and plenty of sun. Fruit trees do not mature overnight; they take years to bear a good crop, but once established (a few years), they almost take care of themselves. Berries yield bountiful crops if soil is good and there is ample sun and water.

Herbs are generally easy to grow, but they too need things: good soil, ample water, and bright light.

The point is that no matter what you grow, you will find that nature is generous. Even if you are a poor gardener, you will have some tomatoes and more than enough berries. The main consideration is taking stock of what space you have for plants and then planning that space to the maximum usage and properly caring for plants.

There is vast wealth in growing plants, not only by saving money but by providing good health and satisfaction. It is nice to eat your own vegetables or homemade honey or top off the day with your own wine. It is more than nice, it is downright satisfying, and in the following chapters we will explore a compendium of green things to grow for pleasure and profit.

4.

Getting Plants Growing

SOWING SEED

⌁ By starting your own vegetables from seeds, you can grow what you want, not just what is available as prestarted plants. The seed-sowing process is relatively easy—it takes more time than experience—and watching your own plants mature is fun and a money-saving experience.

Ironically, years ago seed sowing was even easier than it is today because as more progress has been made in seed development and methods, the procedure has become more complex. Still, sowing seed is not all that hard, so do consider this propagation method.

INDOORS

Let us look at the various ways to start seeds indoors. You can start seed in clay pots or household containers like cottage cheese cartons or aluminum trays frozen rolls come in. Be sure to punch drainage holes in the

bottom of all seed containers. To start seed you need a sterile medium free from disease-causing organisms; vermiculite is the most widely acceptable medium. This lightweight expanded mica product is in packages at nurseries. You can also start seeds in any sterile soil mix or a packaged "starter" mix sold at nurseries.

When you sow seed indoors you get a head start in spring; also, you can sow specific varieties of plants you might want rather than what is generally available at nurseries at seasonal times. Further, some vegetables like eggplant and peas need a long growing season.

To sow seed in vermiculite or starter mixes, use a tray or container at least 3 inches deep. Fill the container to within ½ inch from the top with mix. Now insert seed about ¼ inch into the vermiculite. Water the vermiculite lightly, and cover the container with a plastic Baggie or similiar material to ensure good humidity. Place the seed container in a warm and bright but not sunny place (most seeds germinate at 75° to 78° F.). Remove plastic cover when the first true leaves come up. When the seedling has four leaves transplant it into soil in larger containers. Then put each container in a warm, bright window but not in direct sun, making sure the plants have enough space to grow. Always keep the growing medium moist, never wet or dry.

You can also start seed indoors in more expensive special containers like Jiffy-7 pellets. These pellets are compressed peat disks that contain fertilizer. When the pellets are placed in water, they expand; you put seed inside the expanded disk. Kys Kubes are ready-to-use fiber cubes that contain fertilizer. Water the cube and immediately place the seed directly into the cube. (Fiber pots, trays, and tapes are other ways of starting seeds.) Once seedlings are in cubes or Jiffy pellets, grow them the same way you would seeds in a container. The advantage of the seed pellet and cubes is that there is less shock at transplanting time because the entire block or pellet goes directly into the soil.

Many gardeners start seed indoors under artificial light. If you want to try this method, use Gro-Lux lamps—two tubes to a fixture—and two eight-watt incandescent lamps. Start seeds in trays in starter mix as already prescribed; give plants twelve to sixteen hours of artificial light daily. When the first true leaves appear, transplant them.

No matter which method of starting seed you use, remember that young plants should not go directly from indoors to outdoors. Gradually accustom seeds to outdoor conditions by placing them outside part of the day and bringing them in at night for about three or four nights. In other words, gradually expose seeds to more light and warmth in stages rather than in one swift change.

Outdoors

Many people wait for weather to settle and then start seed directly in the garden. Generally this is fine for most regions of the country, and you can have an excellent vegetable patch in little time. But it is important to start seeds only when weather is absolutely settled; rushing the season can be a disaster. The USDA's map of the last killing frosts for various parts of the country is generally (but not always) safe to follow. Seed packages also have maps on them, telling you when to plant where.

If you are starting seed directly in garden beds, you must first properly condition the soil. You want a crumbly porous soil. Also plants quickly deplete the soil of nutrients, so add organic matter (compost, manure, or rich topsoil) to the soil. The organic matter will make clayey soil more porous and sandy soil more able to retain moisture. At least one third of the plot should be good rich organic matter. Work the matter about 2 inches over the entire plot and then work it into the soil

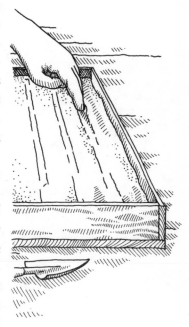

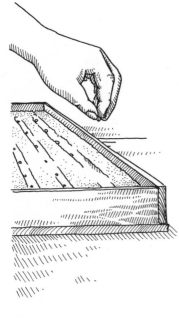

to a depth of at least 4 inches. Finally rake the bed lightly.

You are now ready for seeding the plot. How to arrange the garden? Rows are good, but other planting plans such as edging a flower border or planting in mounds are okay too. Remember that vining plants like cucumbers and squash should be started against fences or trellises they can climb. (This vertical gardening also saves you space.)

There is much mumbo jumbo about how deep to plant seeds in soil; my rule is to plant seed at a depth twice the diameter of the seed. This rule is not rigid because of varying weather and soil conditions. For example, if you have light and dry soil, plant deeper; if the weather is very dry, plant deeper. Also, certain vegetables should be planted at specific depths. Carrots and lettuce, for example, should be started shallow, about ¼ inch into the soil. You can set seeds in place in double rows, in single rows, or in almost any design. Just remember to leave space between seeds so plants can grow and you can tend the plants. And perhaps most important is that you get seeds in the ground at the *right* time, generally, when weather is settled and the danger of frost is over.

Once seeds are in the soil, moisten the soil with a light mist of water. Keep the soil evenly moist while seeds are germinating because dry soil can mean losing half or more of your plants. Also keep weeds out of the garden; hand-pull them as they appear, or wrap some plastic around plants to keep weeds from starting and to prevent water evaporating.

Once plants are growing, thin them out so the strong ones have space to grow. Carrots and beets especially need frequent thinning to produce good crops.

Along with a good soil, the amount of water you give plants will determine whether they grow or die. Vegetables must be grown quickly, so they require lots of water to prosper, which means a thorough soaking to at least 12 inches. To demonstrate how much water soil really needs to produce good crops, consider that thoroughly to soak a 25-square-foot plot to a depth of 12 inches requires about fifteen gallons of water. A hose under normal watering conditions runs about five gallons a minute, so it takes at least fifteen minutes really to soak soil. Thus hand sprinkling will not suffice during the growing months.

PRESTARTS

You can buy prestarted plants at nurseries at seasonal times and save the time and worry of germinating your own seeds. The root crops such as beans, squashes, and peas have to be sown directly where they are to be grown, but tomatoes, peppers, eggplants, and cucumbers are available as prestarts ready for the garden. Vegetables such as lettuce, beets, carrots, and radishes are not available as prestarts because they are so easy to germinate indoors or out.

Start annuals and perennials as seed or prestarts and give these plants the same care as for vegetables.

Prestarted seedlings come in small containers; loosen the plant by wiggling it slightly and ease it from the container. Dig a deep planting hole and insert plant; fill in and around with soil and water thoroughly. Disturb the root ball as little as possible.

PLANTING TREES

If your property has existing fruit or shade trees, use them. You will have to do some pruning and grooming, but usually existing trees can be salvaged. However, if the site does not have any useful trees, and you want some, you must plant them. Most people think planting trees is wasteful because they may not be around when trees mature, but trees grow up in less time than you think, and putting trees on your property is a wise investment: Even if you move, the trees add value to your property if you decide to sell it.

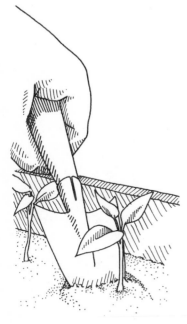

In Chapters 7 and 8 you will find specific information on planting fruit and nut trees. For now, here are some general thoughts to consider. You will probably buy trees from a nursery. The most economical purchase is a young dormant tree that is almost ready to come to life. You should buy a tree about 6 or 8 feet tall: It is still young enough to transplant easily and old enough to be tough, so it can grow. Trees that come in cans can be transplanted at any time when weather is good. Balled and burlapped trees (B&B) are the next good buy and usually easy to transplant in spring or fall. Bare root trees are the least desirable because they take longer to adjust to transplanting; they are usually available in spring and need somewhat more care than canned or B&B trees.

Dig large and deep holes for a tree; a 24-inch depth is good, and the width should be about twice the width of the root ball. Break up soil at the bottom of the hole, and add some topsoil. Give the tree plenty of space because a tree's roots extend almost as far out horizontally as its branches. Set the new plant in place, and fill in and around the tree with fresh soil. Do not feed the plant immediately, but do give it plenty of water. Water slowly and deeply so water gets to the bottom of the roots and in turn stimulates growth.

If you use canned trees, have the nurseryman cut the can so you can easily remove the tree for planting. With balled and burlapped trees, cut the string and spread out the roots.

For the first few weeks, give trees some extra attention. They may need some staking if wind is severe; use piece of wood put in ground tied to the trunk of the tree. Be sure soil is moist, trees are deeply planted, and there are no air pockets in the soil. Once the tree's roots have adjusted to the shock of transplanting, the tree needs only routine care.

FERTILIZERS

There are about fifteen essential elements plants need for nutrition. The three most important elements are nitrogen, phosphorus, and potassium (potash); these are the elements soils most likely lack.

Nitrogen stimulates vegetative development, and it is necessary in the growth of stems and leaves. In early spring, when plants most need nitrogen, it is generally at its lowest content in the soil, for heavy rains have leached it out. Phosphorus is needed in all phases of plant growth, particularly in the production of fruits and seeds; phosphorus also produces good root development. Potassium promotes the general vigor of a plant, making it resistant to certain diseases, and also has a balancing influence on other plant nutrients. Various trace elements such as copper, iron, manganese, sulfur, and zinc are also important to plants.

Most of today's plant foods (fertilizers) are composed of nitrogen, phosphorus, and potassium, with some trace elements. The contents are marked in numbers on the package or the bottle. The first numeral denotes the percentage of nitrogen, the second of phosphorus, and the third of potassium. Fertilizers are available in five forms:

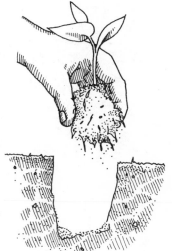

1. *Powdered.* Good, but messy; may stick to foliage, and if stored in a damp place, will cake.

2. *Concentrated liquids.* Use for all fertilizing.

3. *Concentrated powders.* Dilute in water and apply to foliage and plant roots.

4. *Concentrated tablets.* Use mainly for house plants.

5. *Pelleted or granular.* Easy to spread; some granular fertilizers also have insecticides, and others have weed killers.

Besides these man-made fertilizers, there are nitrogen materials to help plants grow. Nitrogen materials, which are water-soluble, can become immediately available to the plant. These materials include ammonium sulfate, ammonium nitrate, urea, nitrate of soda, ammonium phosphate, and calcium nitrate. Results are quick, but they do not last long, and frequent light applications are necessary to obtain uniform growth over a long period of time.

Slowly available nitrogen materials release their nitrogen over relatively long periods. These materials depend upon soil bacteria to decompose and transform the resultant compounds into the nitrogen forms that then become available to the plant. There are two groups of slowly available nitrogen materials: (1) organic matter, which includes sewerage sludge, animal and vegetable tankage, manures, and cottonseed meal; and (2) ureaform compounds, which are synthetic materials made by the chemical union of urea and formaldehyde. Do not confuse urea (quickly available nitrogen) with ureaform.

Plants need feeding when they begin to grow in the spring and while they are making active growth in summer. Generally, woody plants and trees should not be fed after August 1 because this stimulates growth that may not survive fall frosts.

Apply a weak feeding solution frequently rather than one massive dose that might burn roots and foliage. Do not feed new plants; wait a few weeks until they have overcome the shock of transplanting. And do not feed ailing plants because they do not have the capacity to absorb additional food.

To feed vegetables, simply pour or spread fertilizer

on the ground around the plant and lightly scratch it
into the soil or add water, thoroughly, to dissolve the
fertilizer; fertilizer must be in solution for roots to absorb it. Generally, trees are best fed through holes
punched in the ground. Holes are made with a metal
spike, 6 to ·8 feet from the tree trunk. Spikes are removed and then fertilizer is put into the holes, or the
new feeding stakes require only insertion in the ground
and watering; they are already coated with fertilizer.

5.
Vegetables

➹   Today vegetables are easy to grow because hybrid-
izers have produced seeds far superior to those of years
ago. To reiterate what we mentioned in earlier chapters, just what you grow in your vegetable garden depends upon how much time you have for gardening,
your own personal tastes, and how much space you
have. Essentially even a 5×10-foot plot can yield plenty
of vegetables for a family of four. Tomatoes, peppers,
cucumbers, lettuce, radishes, and other delights are
within reach of any gardener with a minimum of effort.
What you ultimately grow will depend on the area of
the United States you live in, and when you plant
specific vegetables is determined by climate. Other con-
siderations are whether vegetables are cool-season or
warm-season. This simply means that some vegetables
need warm weather to grow well, and others grow best
in cooler fall weather. For instance, tomatoes, eggplant,
squash, and cucumbers must be planted when weather

(and soil) is warm, generally in midspring to grow on into summer. On the other hand, cool crops like beets, spinach, lettuce, and cauliflower like areas with cool summers or should be started in midsummer or very early spring to mature before very hot weather starts.

PLANNING THE GARDEN

Do not try to do too much or plan on an extensive vegetable plot the first year. Select some popular vegetables like lettuce, beets, carrots, tomatoes, and beans. This will be enough to whet your appetite and get you going; the following year you can zero in on the more exotic vegetables. In other words, do not try to grow everything all at once.

Successive plantings of different vegetables supply you with a steady supply of foodstuffs. But this requires a lot of planning, work, and time, more than the average gardener cares to do. However, use your allotted space to the best advantage by planting at proper intervals and using wall or fence space or poles for climbing plants like cucumbers and squash. For example, a 10×20-foot garden can accommodate carrots, radishes, tomatoes, cucumbers, and perhaps eggplant and squash. That is enough. But if you want to get energetic regardless of my admonitions, when the vegetables are spent, usually in August or September, use the same plot (revitalized) for winter crops like late cabbage, peppers, chard, and pole beans. Forget about corn (which requires so much space) and potatoes, which are not as easy to grow as you may think.

When planning your vegetable garden, be sure to leave space between rows so you can walk and tend plants. Gardens you have to skip around in are a big bother.

BEANS

Pole beans and bush-type beans are favorite warm-season crops, easy to grow, and usually yield good harvests. Pole beans like to climb, and a good harvest depends on tall plants. The pole beans usually have more flavor and are more productive than the bush beans. For either crop, dig generous holes, and use a rich soil with some compost added to it. Plant seed 1½ inches deep, after the last frost. Fertilize beans with vegetable food and give plants plenty of water.

Pole beans produce in about sixty-five to seventy days and can be picked at various stages of growth; the pods are usually ready about three weeks after blooms. If plants are healthy, you can pick beans every three to five days. Bush beans are ready to harvest in about fifty days.

Hints: Grow pole beans on fences or trellises to save space.

Suggested Varieties
> BUSH-TYPE GREEN BEANS
>> Tendercrop
>> Greensleeves
>> Bush Romano
>
> BUSH-TYPE WAX BEANS
>> Brittle Wax
>> Kinghorn Wax
>
> POLE-SNAP BEANS
>> Kentucky Wonder
>> Blue Lake

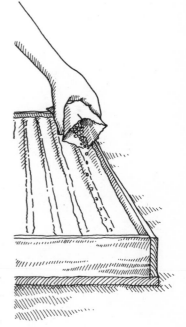

BEETS

Beets are full of good nutrition and can be used for salads or as a cooked vegetable. The tops can be lightly boiled and eaten salted. Plant the seeds ½ inch deep, directly in soil where they will grow, three weeks before the last frost. When seeds are about 2 inches high, thin them so the plants are about 3 inches apart. When plants reach 8 or 9 inches, thin them again by removing every other plant, leaving 3-inch spaces between plants. Beets need sixty days to grow; harvest beets early because if plants are left too long, they become pithy and lose flavor. Small beets have excellent taste.

Beets like a cool temperature and dislike excessive heat, so put them in a shady, somewhat cool location. Fertilize lightly. If plants heave out of the soil, merely add some fresh soil. Keep plants evenly moist because beets like plenty of water.

Hints: Grow beets quickly and pick them when they are young. Give them buckets of water when they are showing good growth.

Suggested Varieties
Early Wonder
Ruby Queen
Detroit Dark Red

BROCCOLI AND CAULIFLOWER

These are cool-weather plants and should be planted in spring a few weeks before the last frost and then again in midsummer. As long as drainage is good these vegetables succeed in almost any soil that has some compost in it. You can start plants indoors or sow seed ¼ inch deep outdoors when weather permits. Space the plants 18 inches apart in rows 28 inches apart. You can also buy plants as prestarts at nurseries. Be sure to water the plants copiously; they should never be dry. With cauliflower, pull outer leaves over the heads to blanch them to keep them white.

Hints: Lots of insects like these vegetables so use routine insect prevention (see page 53).

Suggested Varieties
CAULIFLOWER
Early Snowball
Snow King Hybrid
BROCCOLI
Green Comet
Spartan Early

BRUSSELS SPROUTS

These hardy vegetables can be harvested up to Christmas in most regions. They are best as a fall crop but need a long growing season, so start seed ¼ inch deep indoors in June. Transplant to the garden in July, spacing plants 18 inches apart in rows 28 inches apart. Pinch out lower growing tips when the lower sprouts have reached picking size to make the rest of the sprouts mature. Use a rich fertile soil and keep plants well watered.

Hints: Brussels sprouts are subject to insect attack, so be forewarned.

Suggested Varieties
Jade Cross Hybrid
Long Island Improved

CABBAGE

Cabbage needs space, but it is such an easy crop that I suggest you grow it. Cool-growing, cabbage seed can be sown in the garden but will germinate better if started indoors and transplanted to the garden in early spring, or start plants outdoors in midsummer. If you want fall crops, and cabbage is best grown this way, seed outdoors (as mentioned) in June or July. Space cabbage 15 inches apart and sow seed ¼ inch deep. Give cabbage a deep fertile soil, and be sure it gets plenty of water at all times; never let it dry out.

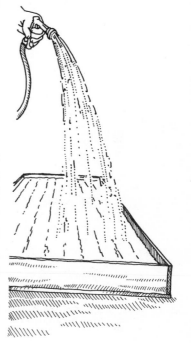

Hints: Cabbage has its share of insect lovers. Hand-pick worms when you see them. Use rotenone when necessary. Harvest when heads are solid and firm.

Suggested Varieties
Golden Acre
Jersey Wakefield
Greenback

CANTALOUPES

Cantaloupes (muskmelons) are fun to grow; they grow fast, and on a trellis they climb and climb. High heat is needed (about 80° to 90° F.) to start melon seeds, but low night temperatures can start rot in plants. Making the transplant is somewhat difficult so this crop should be seeded directly in the garden. Be sure to have manure or compost in the soil, and keep melons plenty moist. Too much rain or cold will produce bad melons. When the melons are ready for harvesting, be sure they have buckets of water, but not so much during the ripening period. A long growing season is needed, about eighty to one hundred days, depending upon variety.

Suggested Varieties
Minnesota Midget
Sugar Baby

CARROTS

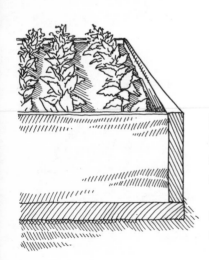

Carrots need a very friable, open soil to prosper. Rapid growth is necessary for good flavor, so frequently feed and water the plants. The longer it takes to mature, the more pithy the carrot will be, which is of course undesirable.

Sow carrot seed in spring or fall, and do not fret if it takes awhile: Many varieties do not germinate for three to four weeks. Plant two rows of carrots, and thin them out when they are about 2 inches tall. Thin the plants again in about one month. Use the thinnings; tiny carrots are delicious. Most varieties require about seventy-five days to become mature. You can resow after harvesting if you want more carrots.

Hints: Carrots are slow to germinate, so do not panic if you do not see green for a while. Once carrots are starting up, be sure to thin them or the crop will be sparse.

Suggested Varieties
Gold Pak
Imperator
Chantenay

CUCUMBERS

Cucumbers are extremely robust, grow quickly, and produce a good harvest. You can sow the seed (buy midget varieties to save space) directly into soil where they are to grow. Insert trellises or stakes so the plants can climb. Train the vine so the center becomes bushy and the lateral stems develop sideways.

Give plants plenty of water, and be sure to add some manure to the soil. Keep plants in a bright place, although direct sun is not necessary. Cucumbers start bearing in about forty to seventy days and can be picked at any stage. The young ones will be tiny but ideal for sweet pickles; larger ones, if you let them mature, are fine for salads.

Suggested Varieties
Bravo Hybrid
Early Surecrop

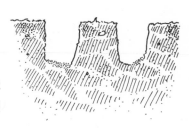

EGGPLANT

A warm-weather plant, eggplant does best at about 80° F. during the day and 68° F. at night. Start seeds

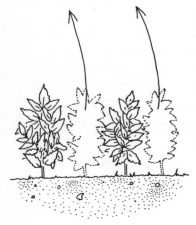

indoors in April or May, depending upon your location, and use peat pots to avoid shock of transplanting. Keep plants well watered and in a bright location.

Plants can be easily trained to a stake or trellis and grow about 3 or 4 feet high, depending upon the variety. As blossoms appear, remove some so eggplant does not set too many fruits. Pinch back terminal stem growth to keep the plant bushy. Eggplant should bear in about seventy days; harvest immediately, even when the fruits are half size; if picked too late, the fruit will have a bitter taste.

Suggested Varieties
   Black Beauty
   Burpee Hybrid

KOHLRABI

This is an easy-to-grow member of the cabbage family. Kohlrabi forms a thick round bulb aboveground where the stem meets the soil. Sow seed in early spring three weeks before last frost (or in summer for fall crops). Put seed ¼ inch deep in rows 24 inches apart and thin to stand 6 inches apart. Kohlrabi needs good light (some sun) and plenty of water to produce abundantly.

Hint: Use kohlrabi cooked as a vegetable or raw in strips to add zest to salads.

Suggested Varieties
   Early White Vienna
   Early Purple Vienna

LETTUCE

The loose-head types of lettuce (leafy ones) are excellent for growing in containers and are ready for plucking within forty-five days. Sow the seed where it is to mature, and protect plants against heat. Give them light, but sun is not necessary to guarantee a crop. Use a 7-40-6 fertilizer, and give lettuce quantities of water once it is growing. Although maturity time is forty-five days, in about one month you can be eating the excellent "thinnings." When lettuce is mature, harvest the outer leaves along with a few inner ones at each cutting. Wash and eat the leaves; you will be amazed at the flavor.

Hints: If you want good lettuce yield, cool weather is the secret. If you grow it through summer, give the crop some shade or use heat-resistant varieties such as Oakleaf and Salad Bowl.

Suggested Varieties
 HEAD LETTUCE
  Great Lakes
  Salad Bowl
 BUTTERHEAD
  Buttercrunch
  Tender Crisp
 LOOSE-LEAF LETTUCE
  Oakleaf
  Salad Bowl

ONIONS

Most people are not inclined to grow onions because they are not a popular cooked vegetable dish nor are they overabundantly used in salads. But the home grower is missing a bet if he does not grow scallions (those sweet-tasting green onions) or chives. These are very easy plants to tend and well worth their space.

You can buy sets or plants of scallions; just set them in the garden or grow them 1 inch apart in a 10-inch pot. Plants will be ready for eating in about forty-five days, at which time you should harvest every other one, leaving the others room to grow until fully developed.

Plenty of water and good sun will bring onions into perfection.

Suggested Varieties
    Evergreen Long White Bunching
    Hardy White Bunching

PEAS

Peas like cool temperatures and are a fairly easy crop to grow, so give them a try. You can get low-growing varieties that do not need staking or trellis types. A fine pea is Mighty Midget, which takes little space and matures in sixty days. Little Marvel, a vine type, is also excellent, maturing in about the same time. Sow seed in pots or tubs, about fifteen peas per square foot, and cover with 1 to 2 inches of soil; or sow directly in garden. Germinated peas need plenty of water; later they do not need as much, but still keep soil moist.

Too hot temperatures will produce all vines, no pods. Watch out for aphids, which cause stunted curly leaves, and pick pods regularly or pods will become hard.

Hints: Start only in cool weather. Use peas fast; pick them as soon as pods are firm.

Suggested Varieties
    TALL-GROWING
    Alderman
    Freezonian
    LOW-GROWING
    Mighty Midget
    Little Marvel

PEPPERS

These attractive plants with dark green foliage can be grown easily in containers as well as in the garden. Peppers need a warm growing period of about two months, with night temperatures never below 65° F.

Planting can be started in April or May (depending upon your region).

There are long and slender hot peppers or the succulent sweet bell peppers. The plants make attractive, bushy, 2- to 3-foot-tall plants. Frequent harvesting will encourage production through the summer.

Hints: Frost quickly kills peppers, so be sure weather is stable before you put plants out. You can harvest peppers at any size.

Suggested Varieties
   GREEN PEPPERS (Sweet)
      Ace Hybrid
      Yolo Wonder
   HOT PEPPERS
      Large Cherry
      Lung Red Cayenne

RADISHES

Radishes are for the rank beginner because no matter how you grow them, they are invariably successful.

As a rule, radishes do not like hot weather, so get them going early in spring. If you water plants thoroughly, and I mean water them, the radishes will be crisp and tender. Fertilize plants when first young leaves appear. Radishes are ready when they taste crisp and succulent, not pithy. The leaves of radishes are a rather decorative note of green; you can replace harvested ones with new seed to have a succession of radishes.

Hint: The easiest vegetable—should grow without any special care in containers or in the garden.

Suggested Varieties
      Burpee White
      Cherry Belle

Spinach

Spinach does best in cool temperatures, rarely making good growth in hot weather, so put it in the coolest location in the garden. In other words, try it in a somewhat shady location. Not as easy to grow as most vegetables, spinach flowers quickly, which stops foliage production. Spinach needs plenty of water to grow successfully. Most varieties mature in about fifty days, making it a tempting fast crop. When you buy spinach, look for blight-resistant varieties, and remember to keep plants thinned to 2 inches apart.

Hints: Start spinach in early spring or in fall because of its preference for coolness. Keep picking spinach; never let plants go to seed.

Suggested Varieties
  Bloomsdale
  America
  Long Standing

Squash

When you grow squash, get ready for a bumper harvest; there will be more than you can consume. A member of the cucumber family, squash is generally easy to grow and will need a support, such as a trellis. Thin plants so you do not have a jungle; try to keep four or five stout stems (per plant) going. Give plants plenty of sun and buckets of water. Once plants are growing, feed them judiciously. Pick squash early and often. There are summer squash varieties and winter varieties; there are also bush types as well as the standard vines.

Hints: Pick squash when young and tender. Borers may attack plants, so dust plants with rotenone in July or August.

Suggested Varieties

SUMMER SQUASH
Cocozelle Bush
Crookneck

WINTER SQUASH
Gold Nugget
Bush Ebony

TOMATOES

There are few things that beat the sweet luscious taste of freshly picked tomatoes. And tomatoes are usually successful even for the neophyte gardener to grow.

Tomatoes need warm temperatures and as much sun as possible to produce a good crop. They are climbers and so need to be staked; that is, insert trellises or wood stakes into the soil and fasten plants to the wood members with tie-ons.

Give tomato plants plenty of water and good feeding with a tomato-type food (sold at nurseries). Keep the plants growing continuously so you have a good harvest. Fertilize first about one week after you transplant the seedlings and again in about two weeks. While plants are producing fruit, fertilize every week.

You can pollinate tomato blossoms by shaking the plant (assuming there are no bees in the area). New blossoms open daily over a long period of time. Keep tomatoes at temperatures above 60° F. at night or they may not set fruit. Very warm temperatures, over 95° F., will affect plants, so shelter plants from extreme sun on very hot days.

Thin tomato plants by removing the small suckers as they form. These are the tiny first two or three leaves that appear between the main stem and the foliage. Depending upon the variety, tomatoes should bear within seventy to eighty days after seed planting.

Hints: Stake tomatoes; tie the plants to wooden stakes. Remove suckers that develop in axils of main leaf stalks. If tomato hornworms attack, use Sevin. Pick tomatoes as soon as they are red; green-picked tomatoes ripened indoors are okay but do not have the flavor of tomatoes ripened on the vine.

Suggested Varieties
EARLY
    Early Hybrid
    Spring Giant
MIDSEASON
    Heinz
    Marglobe
SMALL AND MIDGET
    Red Cherry
    Tiny Tim

TURNIPS

Turnips are often neglected by gardeners and yet they are excellent nutrition as a cooked vegetable, especially in stews. The turnip must make its quick growth in early spring or late fall. Sow seed in spring six weeks before last frost date or in midsummer. Put seed $\frac{1}{2}$ inch deep in rows 20 inches apart. Thin out seedlings to stand 3 inches apart. Use a loose well-drained soil, and plant turnips in bright light. Turnips need even moisture.

Hints: The variety Tokyo Cross matures up to fifteen days earlier than most varieties. Turnips can be stored over winter in a box of sand in a cool basement.

Suggested Varieties
    Just Right
    Tokyo Cross

PLANTING SCHEDULE FOR VEGETABLES

Vegetable	Planting-Out Time Seeds	Planting-Out Time Transplants	Distance Between Rows	Space Apart in Rows	Seed Depth	Growing Days Needed in Garden	Comments
Beans, snap	After last frost		24-30"	33"	1 1/2"	50	For shell beans also, but leave on bush until pods dry.
Beans, pole	After last frost		60"	5" (12")*	1 1/2"	65	Pole limas will be 2 weeks later. Trellis required for all.
Beets	3 weeks before last frost		10-20"	1" (3")	1/2"	60	Beet tops are excellent cooked or as salad greens.
Winter-keeper	By mid-July		10-20"	1" (3")	1/2"	80	This is a special variety for fall crop and good winter storage.
Broccoli and cauliflower		4 weeks before last frost	28"	18"	1/4"	50 after transplanting	Sow indoors 6 weeks before planting-out time. Guard against cabbage loopers, harlequin bugs, and cabbage-family pests.
Brussels sprouts		4 weeks before last frost	28"	18"	1/4"	80 after transplanting	Start same as broccoli for spring. Good for fall crop.
Cabbage		4 weeks before last frost	28"	15"	1/4"	60-70 after transplanting	Start same as broccoli for spring. Good for fall crop. Watch for cabbage loopers (see Broccoli).

*Figure in parenthesis indicates space apart in row after thinning.

Vegetable	Planting-Out Time		Distance Between Rows	Space Apart in Rows	Seed Depth	Growing Days Needed in Garden	Comments
	Seeds	Transplants					
Cabbage Chinese (fall crop)	By mid-July		28"	3-4" (12")*	1/2"	70	Can tolerate light frosts, but harvest before heavy freeze. Excellent in fall.
Carrots	2 weeks before last frost or after		20"	1/4" (3")	1/4"	75	Late carrots can be kept in ground all winter under mulch.
Cucumbers	After last frost		48"	4" (12")	1/2"	40-70	Cucumbers grow well on fences, trellises (save space).
Eggplant		After last frost	36"		1/4"	70 after transplanting	Sow indoors 8 weeks before planting-out time.
Kohlrabi	3 weeks before last frost		24"	1" (6")	1/4"	55	Guard against same insects as attack broccoli, cabbage. Better than turnip for spring crop in hot-summer areas.
Lettuce, leaf	5 weeks before last frost		16"	1/2" (2")	1/4"	45	Thinnings make excellent early salads. Most dependable.
Lettuce, butterhead	5 weeks before last frost		18"	1/2" (6")	1/4"	75	May be handled like head lettuce if desired. Small, delicious.

*Figure in parenthesis indicates space apart in row after thinning.

Vegetable	Planting-Out Time Seeds	Planting-Out Time Transplants	Distance Between Rows	Space Apart in Rows	Seed Depth	Growing Days Needed in Garden	Comments
Lettuce, head		3 weeks before last frost	18"		1/4"	85	Sow in coldframe 4 weeks before planting-out time. Stands heat better than butterhead type.
Melons (cantaloupes, watermelon)	1 week after last frost		60"	6" (at least 18")*	1"	80–100	In short-season areas use quick-maturing varieties; plants may be prestarted indoors in peat pots.
Onion, sets		Early as ground is prepared	15"		1 1/2" - 2"	45	One-pound average sets should plant about 50-foot row. Medium to small sets are better than large ones.
Onion, plantlets		Early as ground is prepared	15"			120	Used to gain time for production of bulb onions for storage.
Onion, bunching, or others from seeds	2 weeks before last frost or after		15"	1/2" (bulb types to 4")	1/2"	100 or more	Use fresh seed. Bunching onions may remain in garden over winter.
Peas	6 weeks before last frost		30"	2–3"	1"	63	May be grown on low trellis.
Peppers		After last frost	36"		1/4"	70	Start seeds indoors 8 weeks before planting-out date.

*Figure in parenthesis indicates space apart in row after thinning.

Vegetable	Planting-Out Time		Distance Between Rows	Space Apart in Rows	Seed Depth	Growing Days Needed in Garden	Comments
	Seeds	Transplants					
Radishes	4 weeks before last frost		12"	1/2" (1")*	1/4"	25	For prolonged prime supply, make successive sowings 2 weeks apart, spring and fall.
Spinach	3 weeks before last frost		15"	1/2" (2")	1/2"	48	A cool-weather crop. "Bolts" (goes to seed) in hot weather.
Spinach, New Zealand	1 week before last frost		28"	1" (5")	1/2"	50	Better for hot-summer areas than regular spinach.
Squash, bush or vine	After last frost		60" between groups	3 plants per group, 18" apart	1"	Summer types 52; winter types 85-115	Where space is limited, use bush type.
Tomatoes		After last frost	48"		1/2"	70 from transplanting	Sow seeds indoors 6 weeks before planting-out date. Staked plants may be spaced closer than unstaked ones. Late-crop tomatoes may be seeded directly in ground.
Turnips	(Spring) 6 weeks before last frost. (Fall) 10 weeks before first expected frost		20"	3/4" (3")	1/2"	55	Good fall crop, stores well.

*Figure in parenthesis indicates space apart in row after thinning.

INSECTS

The first line of defense is observation. If you see a few aphids or mealybugs, you can eradicate them quickly without much trouble. But once insects get a foothold you are in trouble; sprays, chemicals, and all other kinds of insidious means will be necessary to save your plants. Prevention is nine tenths the battle of keeping vegetables healthy, so be alert and on guard.

Aphids are tiny, oval, soft-bodied pests; mealybugs are cottony masses hard to miss; and scale are hard-shelled insects that attach themselves to plants and somewhat resemble apple seeds. All these insects are easy to see and easy to get rid of if you catch them early. The one insect you will not be able to see that is liable to attack vegetables is spider mite; you must hope that your plants are not attacked by this culprit. Dry air is a common cause of spider mite.

Vegetables (depending upon the kind) will attract other unwanted visitors, although they may never appear if you keep a clean house. Chewing insects of various kinds love leafy vegetables, so keep rotenone insecticide on hand. Hookworms and cutworms may appear on tomatoes—hand-pick and destroy them, or use Sevin (only one or two applications are needed). Cucumber beetles are easily discouraged from squash and cucumbers by using a regular rotenone or Pyrethrum insecticide. If you are growing beans, watch for bean leaf beetles or Mexican bean beetles; use Sevin.

Squash borers can wipe out a good crop; if you see them, dust with rotenone, especially in early June to about mid-July. Snails and slugs love vegetables. Use snail and slug bait; Corys is the best if you can find it, but if not, try Bug-Geta. Sprinkle pellets on the soil. Use these chemicals and all insecticides with care and only as detailed on the package. It is especially important in any type of vegetable garden to observe caution on labels about discontinuing use a certain length of time before harvest.

The chart that follows will help you select appropriate remedies to combat bugs. In the main, I have tried to select preventatives that are non-accumulative in the soil, and while these are still poisons they are less toxic than most other remedies. Of course, when you use insecticides, follow directions on the package or bottle carefully and keep all poisons out of reach of children or pets.

If you object to using poisons around the home see Chapter 12, which includes some old-fashioned remedies which do not include chemicals.

DISEASES

Diseases rarely attack plants in containers, but in the yard some of the common diseases like blight, bacterial spot, and fusarium wilt may occur. Again, do not panic, because there are some excellent preventatives. But like insects that have favorite foods, diseases attack certain crops too. Many vegetable varieties are disease-resistant; look for them when buying seeds because they are certainly worth the search.·

Here is a chart that summarizes what you should know about diseases that attack vegetables.

Once you have identified the specific disease you will find remedies at local nurseries. These preventatives are sold under various trade names, too many to list.

DISEASE CHART

Disease	Vegetable Attacked	Damage
Bacterial blight	Beans	Water-soaked spots on leaves
Mosaic	Beans	Mottled leaves
Anthracnose	Beans Cucumbers Squash	Sunken, reddish brown to blackish spots; red areas on leaves
Fusarium wilt	Cucumbers Squash Tomatoes	Red areas on leaves
Fusarium yellows	Cabbage Cauliflower Broccoli Cucumbers Squash	Leaves turn yellow
Leaf blight	Carrots	Outer leaves turn yellow
Aster yellows	Carrots	Inner leaves stunted, yellow
Powdery mildew	Peas	White to grayish coating on leaves
Wilt	Peas Tomatoes	Yellow, dwarfed plants; plants stunted
Bacterial spot	Tomatoes Peppers Eggplant	Scabby spots on fruit
Blight (many types and kinds)	Many crops	Leaves affected in various ways; spots, rings, streaks
Viruses	Many crops	Leaves mottled or spotted in patterns

INSECT SPRAY SCHEDULE FOR VEGETABLES

Vegetable	Pest	Preventative	When to Spray
Beans	Mexican bean beetle. Orange to yellow, with black spots on back. Larvae fuzzy, 1/3 inch long. Feeds on pods and underside of leaves.	Rotenone	When larvae or adult begins to feed. Repeat once at 7 to 10 day interval.
Beets	Leaf miner. Slender, gray, black-haired fly, 1/4 inch long. Larvae pale green, make blotches in leaves.	Diazinon Malathion	When first blisters appear in leaves. Repeat once at 7 to 10 day interval.
Broccoli Brussels sprouts	Maggots. Yellowish white, legless worms, less than 1/2 inch long; tunnel in roots.	Diazinon	Transplanting time.
Cabbage Cauliflower	Cabbage looper. Pale green worm to 1 1/2 inches long. Chews holes in leaves.	Sevin Malathion	When young worms begin to feed. Repeat every 5 to 7 days until week before harvest.
Cucumbers	Cucumber beetles, flea beetles, leafhoppers. Eat foliage.	Sevin	At 7- to 10-day intervals when insects appears. (Avoid spraying open blossoms.)
Eggplant	Eggplant lacebug. Grayish to brown, flat, with lacelike wings. Sucks juices; leaves yellow.	Malathion	Use every 7 days.
Lettuce	Aphids. Suck juices, causing leaves to yellow.	Malathion	When insects appear, and weekly as needed.

Vegetable	Pest	Preventative	When to Spray
Onion	Thrips. Tiny, yellow or brown, winged insects. Larvae white, wingless. Both suck juices, causing white blotches on leaves.	Malathion	When leaves begin to be scarred. Repeat 2 to 3 times.
Peas	Aphids.	Malathion	When insects appear.
	Weevil. Brown with white or black markings, 1/3 inch long. Larvae white, small, to 1/3 inch.	Rotenone	When plants blossom and before pods form.
Spinach	Leaf miner.	Same as beets.	Same as beets.
	Aphids.	Same as beets.	When plants are young, before leaves curl, discontinue 7 days before harvest.
Squash	Cucumber beetles, flea beetles, leafhoppers.	Same as cucumbers.	Same as cucumbers.
Swiss chard	Same as beets.	Same as beets.	Same as beets.
Tomatoes	Cutworms. Dull gray, brown, or black worms.	Sevin Diazinon	Apply pesticide to soil surface around plants when setting out.
	Hornworms. Large green worms, to 4 inches.	Sevin	Use every 7 days.
	Aphids and mites.	Malathion Kelthane	When pests appear.

Note: When using any insecticide or fungicide check label to determine when to stop using before harvest. (Generally, it is 1 to 2 weeks).

6.
Herbs

These plants, valuable in salads and cooking, can really grow on their own and need no special preparation, so in this chapter we will concentrate on some basic herbs rather than detailed information on how to grow them.

I grow herbs all over the property, wherever space is available, because if there is sun, herbs will grow. Parsley is tucked amid the cosmos. Tarragon decks the vegetable patch, and dill grows wild at the bottom of my land. Of course, if you want a special place—all herbs together—make a planting design in neat rows or circles or whatever pleases you.

You can buy herbs as prestarts at nurseries, or sow seeds of most herbs as soon as the last spring frost is over.

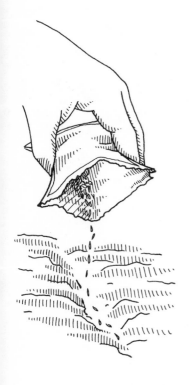

HERBS TO GROW AND KNOW

BASIL

This annual plant is almost a basic ingredient in Italian cooking. There are many types of basil, from the wide-leaved kinds to the coppery ones, but basically most people grow sweet basil, which is fine. Sweet basil grows to about 24 inches and needs really good sun. Plants in the garden will set seed, so you will have more plants the following summer.

DILL

You can do more with this annual herb than you think. For instance, use dill dried on boiled artichokes for a pleasant taste treat. Dill is feathery and ferny in appearance, and its only drawback in the garden is that it grows tall, to about 6 feet. The small yellow flowers are borne in clusters. Whenever the weather is warm you can sow seeds of dill in the garden; dill will tolerate some shade if necessary. Plants seed themselves.

MARJORAM

This is a good herb for salads, fish dishes, and some meats. Marjoram is a perennial plant that generally lives over, but I find it just as easy to seed new plants each year. In spring, when the weather is safely warm, seed marjoram in a sunny place; plants grow to about 20 inches and are rather attractive in the garden.

PARSLEY

Try to get the plain-leaved parsley rather than the curly-leaved; the curly-leaved parsley looks prettier in the garden, but the plain-leaved type has more flavor. Parsley is a biennial that comes back the second year after seeding. This is the one herb that needs attention: a constantly moist bed for germination. Start plants indoors under controlled conditions. Plants will grow in bright light without too much sun if they have to, but the more sun the better.

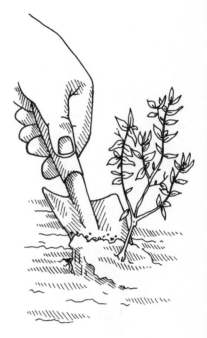

ROSEMARY

If you have space, grow some rosemary because it is good in fish dishes and as a medicinal herb. Cuttings root easily, or plant seed. Plants grow to about 36 inches. There are both upright and creeping varieties of rosemary.

SAGE

This perennial has gray-green leaves and pretty purple and white flowers. Plants will grow in a sunny place, even in poor soil. Although sage is not as popular as most herbs, it does have its uses in poultry stuffing.

SAVORY

There are both summer savory and winter savory; summer savory is a delicate-looking plant with a few leaves, and winter savory is big, with dark green leaves and pretty white flowers. Both winter and summer savory need a sunny spot, and both are good for vegetable dishes and poultry stuffing.

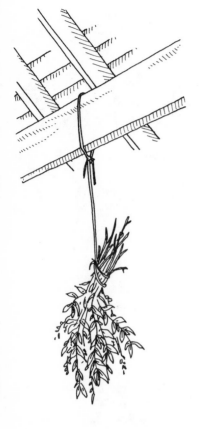

Tarragon

This is a favorite culinary herb, but get the right kind of tarragon: *Artemisia dracunculus*. My best tarragon grows in a somewhat shady place, although most herb experts say it does better in full sun. Tarragon is especially good for vinegars and as a sauce with white wine and butter for liver or fish.

Thyme

This perennial plant adds a nice taste to dishes with eggs, or use thyme as a tea. There are several varieties. Give plants sun.

DRYING HERBS

Gather herbs early in the morning, when plants have just started to bloom, if you want the best flavor. Dry herbs in the sun or in the oven, or just let them hang in loose bunches in a cool dry attic. When dry, strip off leaves and bottle the herbs in clean, dry, labeled jars.

If you want to oven-dry herbs, place them on cookie sheets and cover them with waxed paper; heat oven to 130° F., until the herbs are brittle to the touch. For sun drying, pick a warm dry day and put plants on trays that have underneath ventilation. A screened box is ideal: Make this tray from four pieces of soft wood and some hardware cloth (mesh screen). Turn the herbs a few times so all parts get dry. When herbs are brittle to the touch, strip and bottle them.

For drying herbs in an attic, tie herbs into loose bunches and hang them upside down from rafters or nails in the ceiling. When leaves are brittle, strip them off and bottle the herbs.

7.
Fruit Trees

Fruit trees not only have lovely blossoms and fresh green leaves in spring, but they also produce fruit. Nothing equals the taste of fruit fresh from the tree, and, as a dividend, if you cannot eat all the fruit from the trees, you can preserve what is left over for future pleasure. If you already have fruit trees on the property you are indeed lucky, but if you do not have any, I urge you to grow some. Once planted and growing, fruit trees need no more care than a house plant; fruit trees do *not* require acres of land—you can have fruit trees even in a small garden. For example, in an area 150 feet long and 50 feet wide I have cherry, peach, apricot, and apple trees.

GETTING STARTED WITH FRUIT TREES

If you are starting your own trees, you will want to know how long it takes plants to bear. Bearing time is determined by the fruit and the variety. For example, I have five different varieties of apple trees, and each bear fruit at different times during the year: the first in May, the last in October or November. Generally apple and pear trees require from four to six years to come to bearing; peach, plum, and cherry trees take three or four years. Miniature varieties vary somewhat in their bearing time. This information is generally listed in catalogs, or your local nurseryman can tell you the time.

Individual regional climates dictate just what fruit trees you can grow; plant only the fruits and varieties that will endure the seasons of your area. The trees must be hardy enough to stand the coldest winter and the hottest summer of your vicinity. Generally, the local nursery you buy trees at (and this is the best place to buy from) will stock only those varieties that do well in your area. Select the variety you want; for example, some apples are excellent for eating, whereas others are better for cooking or preserving. And some varieties, like the McIntosh, are good for both eating and cooking. (A few trees of each type would be nice, but this is probably impossible because of space.) For apples and pears you will have to determine whether you want early, mid-season, or late varieties of fruits.

All fruits do have limits as to what region they can be grown in; few will do well out of their proper climate, so use northern types for the North and southern types for the South. Also remember that many varieties of fruit trees are self-sterile, which means that they will not set a crop unless other plants that blossom at the same time and furnish pollen are nearby. Make sure

that either the proper cross-pollination is provided for
or that the variety you are buying is self-fruiting.

BUYING TREES

As mentioned, if possible buy from local nurseries because most are reliable, and rarely sell a dormant tree
that will not survive if properly planted. If you buy
from a mail-order house, find out the tree's season, its
hardiness, whether it is best grown in the North or
South, whether it is meant for cooking or eating, and,
most importantly, its resistance to diseases and insects.
In other words, do not just buy any old tree because it
is a fruit tree—be discriminating, just as you would
with other items you purchase.

Ideally you should buy one- or two-year-old trees because they are the best buy for the beginner. Most stone
fruits are sold when one year old; apple and pear trees
are generally sold when they are about two years old.
Get trees that are stocky and branching rather than
spindly and compact. Let your nurseryman guide you
to a certain extent, and then use your eyes to determine
a well-proportioned tree.

Whether you buy from a local source or a mail-order
supplier, if possible plant trees at once. If there must be
a delay, "heel in" the trees. This is temporary planting:
dig a shallow trench wide and deep enough to hold the
trees' roots, set the plants on their sides, and cover the
roots with soil and water them. Try to keep the new
trees out of blazing sun and soaring wind.

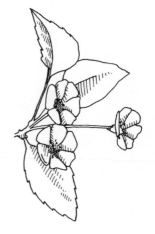

PLANTING TREES

Even a half-dozen trees can be grouped as ornamen-
tals in a garden no larger than a quarter acre, so do not
worry too much about the number of trees you are
planting. Also do not brood over planting distances.
Experts usually maintain that apple trees require 30 to

40 feet planting distance. But my apple, pear, and peach trees are only 15 or 20 feet apart and yet are prospering and bearing fruit.

For the average gardener, tree arrangement is not very important. I have ten fruit trees in an arc arrangement in the front of the house, four trees in another area in a different arrangement, and about twelve trees at the back of the house in yet another form. I have a good supply of apples, peaches, apricots, pears, plums, and cherries—what else could one want? I firmly believe that it is much more important to prepare the land for the tree than to fret about planting distances and arrangements.

Prepare the ground for your fruit trees with care. You want a friable and workable soil, one with air. Dry sandy soil will not hold water, and clayey soil will not drain properly. To have a friable soil that drains, you usually have to add lots of organic matter to the existing soil. Compost yourself, or buy sacks of compost. Turn over the soil and add your organic matter, working it well into the soil. Do a little at a time until the soil is crumbly and rich. This may seem like a lot of work, but it is essential because it will save you much work later.

Plant the trees in fall or spring when the land is warm and mellow, and hope for good spring showers and sun to get the plants going. Dig holes for new trees deep enough to let you set the plant in place as deep as it stood at the nursery. Make the diameter of the hole wide enough to hold the roots without crowding. When you dig the hole, put the surface soil on one side and the subsoil on the other side so the richer topsoil can be put back in the hole directly on the roots. Pack the soil in place firmly, but do not pack it down tightly by tramping on it—you want the soil somewhat loose to prevent evaporation. Water plants thoroughly, but do not feed them because they are not yet ready for it. Fertilizers must be used sparingly, if at all, in the first year.

Some experts insist that you prune fruit trees; others say not to. Usually a *sparse* pruning is all that is necessary. Only peach trees seem to benefit from severe pruning. Give your fruit trees some extra care the first year: Make sure they are growing straight (stake them if necessary), and watch the color of the foliage, which will indicate what is going on in the tree. Any change from luxuriant green to yellow means something is awry—the chlorophyll in the foliage is not functioning well. Small or few leaves are other signs of something wrong.

Keeping Trees Growing

The cultivation of home fruit trees requires some attention to water, sun, feeding, pruning, and insect protection. You cannot do much about the sun, but in a normal year there most likely will be plenty of sunlight to keep your trees growing well. If there are ample rains, you will not have to water extensively; if it is a dry year, you will. Actively growing trees need feeding about twice a year with a standard 10-10-5 plant food or one specifically made for fruit trees. Pruning and spraying are probably the most important functions you will have to do. Pruning increases a plant's vigor. Leaves and shoots need a constant supply of nutrients, so when you decrease the size of the plant top, the remaining parts grow more vigorously. A general good rule of pruning is to keep a slender habit of growth. Do not let the tree get too drooping or spreading; prune slightly but judiciously. Peach and apple trees can take more pruning than pear or cherry trees. The stone fruits, especially the peach, bear fruit on the previous year's growth, so every year the new crop is borne farther and farther from the trunk if you do not prune. More pruning keeps the bearing wood near the trunk. Apple and pear trees bear fruit on spurs on wood two or more years old, so intense pruning is not necessary.

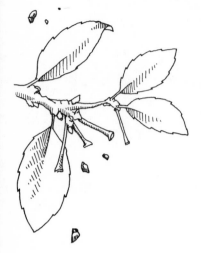

Fruit trees are subject to pests and occasionally to disease, but a dormant oil spray applied in the early spring will discourage the culprits. These prepared sprays are sold at nurseries. Because pest problems vary greatly from one state to another, ask your Agricultural Extension Service for a spraying schedule and a list of which preventatives to use. Generally, apply a dormant oil spray when leaves are about ¼ inch long. Then use an all-purpose fruit spray when blossoms show color, again when the last petals are falling, and every ten days thereafter until two weeks before harvesting. (See spray schedule for insects at end of chapter.)

INDIVIDUAL FRUIT TREES

Apple

Apple trees, the hardiest of fruit trees, can be grown in every state but Florida. Apple trees can tolerate a wide variety of climates; there are some apple trees that will even tolerate −20° F. The ideal climate for apple trees is somewhat cool, with plenty of sun and abundant rainfall. Choose the variety best suited for your climate. Remember, varieties that thrive in North Atlantic states may not grow in the South.

There are so many varieties of apple trees that it is hazardous to suggest the best ones for each area, but the hardiest trees for really cold climates and short seasons are Wealthy, Yellow Transparent, and Alexander. The next hardiest group are McIntosh and Milton. In the cold Northeast, Baldwin, Gravenstein, and Jonathan excel, and for milder climates such as regions south of New York, Delicious and Winesap are always good.

Apple trees grow best in a well-drained, almost neutral soil, with a pH of about 6.5 to 7.0. In fact, in most areas the existing soil will be fine for apple trees, so there is no need to worry about pH testing. Standard-size apple trees still get my vote, but if your space is limited, grow dwarf or semidwarf trees. Put in dwarf varieties about 10 feet apart, standards about 30 feet. Good robust two-year-old trees are the best buy. Put trees in the ground with only very light pruning, a branch here or there.

Once trees are growing, apply light feeding about three or four times in the warm seasons. Too much fertilizer can promote foliage growth but may impair the size of the crop.

Apple trees bear so heavily that branches cannot support the fruit, so thin out fruit sometime in June.

Apple insects include aphids, leaf rollers, apple maggots, and scale; diseases are apple scab and fire blight.

Apricot

Most apricot trees will bear fruit if planted alone, but some, such as Sungold, need two trees for cross-pollination. The best way to be sure is to ask the nurseryman. Grow apricot trees in a neutral soil. These plants can be grown in most regions except in severe-winter areas where temperature goes below −30° F. Space standard-sized trees 10 to 15 feet apart, dwarfs about 6 feet apart. Prune the trees slightly when you put them in the ground, and every year remove deadwood and overcrowded branches. I prune somewhat more severely because the apricot can be shaped into a most handsome tree, and I like its ornamental value in the landscape. Apricot trees will need some feeding once trees are established; 10-10-10 is a satisfactory food.

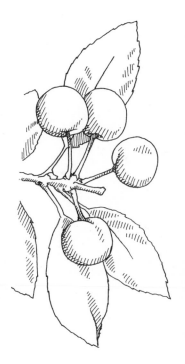

Apricot trees are easy to grow and pull their own weight on the grounds. Just make sure you start the young trees properly, as outlined in the beginning of the chapter. Apricot trees live about thirty years, never get tall enough to be overpowering, and make fine trees for your property.

Apricot trees are infected by red mites and scale if you do not care for them.

CHERRY

Cherries are an overlooked but delightful crop available in sour or sweet types. The sweet cherries—Bing and Queen Anne—are delicious for out-of-hand eating; the sour cherries are the ones for preserves, jams, pies, and so forth and are much hardier and easier to grow than the sweet ones. Generally cherry trees do well under the same climatic conditions as apple trees. Sour cherry trees bear in the fourth or fifth year; sweet cherry trees bear a few years later. There are bush-type cherry trees to 6 to 8 feet (I have never grown these) and standard-sized trees to 25 feet.

Make sure that the cherry trees you buy are double-bearing, or pollination will be difficult. Check with your local nurseryman.

Cherry trees require good light, so be sure to prune trees properly every year; prune so that five or six limbs of your cherry tree become the main bearing limbs. Leave a single top growing straight up as a leader, but trim other branches so they are shorter than the leader. You want growth to have plenty of open space and good vertical shape.

Cherry trees more than any other fruit trees just will not tolerate a wet soil, so drainage is of the utmost importance. The pH of the soil should be above neutral, about 8.0. When you plant the tree, remove all but four of the best branches. The trees will tolerate a light feeding now and then through the summer (10-10-10) but in general do not need too much additional food.

Cherry trees attract birds, who will eat the cherries. Netting is one ugly solution; hope that birds arrive after

the cherries develop or that the cherries arrive before
the birds find them. But the best decoy, if you have the
time and fortitude, is to plant a mulberry tree—birds
like mulberries even better than cherries.

Cherry trees are prone to attacks by aphids, scale,
and mites. Brown rot is the disease most likely to infect
plants.

PEACH

Peach trees provide not only a genuine taste treat but
also a genuine patience problem. Peach trees will grow
in almost all parts of the country, but they are temperamental, maybe bearing heavily one year but little the
next year. Peach trees need both cold (below 40° F.)
and warmth; however, one cold snap can wipe out
some peach trees, and fruit is sparse without summer
warmth! In spite of all their problems, peach trees are
worth every effort because they supply fruit that is im-
measurably good and unlike any you can buy at a
market.

Buy the peach varieties that will tolerate your climate (there are thousands of varieties). Most peach
trees are self-pollinating, but to be sure you get fruit,
have two or three peach trees. Peach trees will bear in
about four years. I do not encourage pruning most fruit
trees at initial planting, but peach trees need some
pruning because they do not take well to transplanting.
Prune the tops to encourage root development so the
tree gets a good start. Cut the leader (center) branch
slightly and all other branches to about 4 inches. Prune
trees slightly yearly; only at planting should you prune
severely.

Peach trees grow best in neutral soil, bearing within
three to four years. Plant trees in early spring, cutting
them back 2 to 3 feet above ground level, leaving three
or four strong branches; let one branch develop into a
"leader."

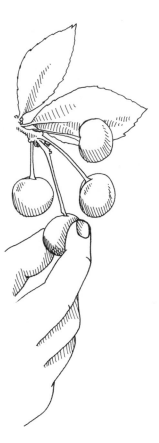

Peach trees seem to react favorably to feeding, so use a 10-10-10 plant food applied every other watering.

The dwarf peach Bonanza is a very popular tub plant, but do not expect too much from it; mine had fruit for a few years and then gave out. Other gardeners have told me that the same thing happened to them.

Peach trees are subject to leaf curl and brown rot and aphids, moths, scale, and mites. Keep the area around the trunk of the tree (where bacterial diseases may start) free of debris.

Pear

Pear trees need a good winter chill to be at their best and will grow in the same regions as apple and peach trees. Pear trees flower earlier than apple trees, so frost may be a problem. Pear trees will do fairly well even in a poor soil *if* the soil has good drainage. Buy pear trees in different varieties to ensure pollination (although trees are mostly self-fertile). Pear trees need almost no pruning, so you do not have to worry about them at pruning time as you do with apple or peach trees.

Pear trees come standard-sized or dwarfed. Standard trees bear in their fifth year, dwarfs in the third year. Cut back young standard trees to 3 feet at planting time. Train the trees as they grow; once the skeleton is established, pruning is no longer necessary.

Pear trees will do well in a somewhat heavier soil than most fruit trees. Feeding is really not necessary if soil is good; watch leaves for signs of lack of food: If leaves are pale or yellow-green, apply a weak fertilizer.

Do not let pears ripen on the tree or they will develop brown centers and soft flesh. Pick pears when they are slightly green.

Fire blight is the nemesis of pear trees and it can strike all parts of the tree; fire blight scorches parts of plants. Trim any blighted area *as soon as you see it*. Do not wait. The worst time for blight is from bloom to fruit, so watch plants closely during this period.

PLUM

Plum trees need a good winter chill to bear profusely and can be grown in those parts of the United States where temperatures do not drop below $-20°$ F. Select a locally adapted variety. Plums are valuable because they preserve well and supply you with lots of prunes. Prune plums are best for this, although regular plums are sometimes used too.

Most plum trees are self-fertile, so you will not need two varieties. Fall planting is better where winters are mild enough, but spring planting is satisfactory too. Prune trees so they are wide open and spreading. As with cherry trees, birds are the main nemesis of plum trees rather than diseases or insects, so net trees or plant mulberry trees.

SPRAY SCHEDULE FOR FRUITS

Tree	When to Spray	Pest	Preventatives
Apple	1. Green-tip stage: When blossom buds are opening	Aphids, scale, mites, redbugs	Superior oil, 60 or 70 viscosity
	2. Petal-fall stage: After petals fall	Codling moth, curculio, leaf roller, canker worm, mites, tent caterpillar, scab	Malathion/Captan*
	3. Second application 10 days after petals fall	Same as above	Same as above
	4. Third application 2 weeks after second application	Same as above	Same as above
Cherry	1. Delayed dormant: When the leaves of the blossom ends are out 1/4 inch	Black cherry aphids, European red mites, scale	Superior oil, as for apples
	2. First application: When buds begin to show color	Aphids, mites, brown rot	Malathion/Captan*
	3. Second application: When last petals are falling	Aphids, mites, curculio, brown rot	Same as above
Peach	1. Before buds show any green at the tip	Leaf curl disease	Ferbam
	2. Before fruit bud development	Aphids, red mites, cottony peach scale	Superior oil
	3. Petal-fall	Curculio, mites, fruit moths, brown rot, scab	Malathion/Captan*

Tree	When to Spray	Pest	Preventatives
Pear	1. Green-tip stage	Psylla and leaf blister mites	Superior oil, as for apples
	2. When petals fall	Psylla, blister mite, scab	Malathion/Captan*
	3. Another application 2 weeks after petal-fall	Same as above	Same as above
Plum Apricot	1. Green tip stage: when blossom buds are opening	European red mites, European fruit lecanium, San Jose scale	Superior oil, as for apples
	2. When last petals fall	Same as peach	Malathion/Captan*

Do not use insecticide on any fruit tree during flowering period. Combination sprays for fruits come ready-mixed at nurseries.

8.
Nut Trees

❧ A good nut tree is like a valuable investment: Nuts are high in protein, and most nut trees are handsome and can be used as shade trees in gardens. Nut trees are inevitably easier to grow than fruit trees and once established are like money in the bank. (Note though that nut trees take years to mature.) For the most part there are nut trees for all parts of the country, although soft-shelled almonds do not bear in very cold climates (hard-shelled almonds do).

Nut trees, like fruit trees, need good drainage and ample water through the years, and a northern or eastern slope is the best site for most nut trees. Many varieties of nut trees are hardy throughout the United States, although, as with fruit trees, some varieties are best planted in specific regions: The pecan, for example, is primarily a southern tree. Check with your local nurseryman for the best varieties for your region.

Most nut trees need light pruning yearly, but if pruning is neglected, trees will still grow well once es-

tablished. A dormant oil spray will help keep down insects, although once established, nut trees are rarely bothered by insects.

Nut trees will, if necessary, grow in almost any soil, but ideally well-drained loose subsoils are best because nut trees are mostly deep-rooted trees and a soil that contains organic matter helps retain moisture between rains. Avoid swampy or rocky soils—practically no plant will grow in such soil. Neutral or slightly acid soils are best for almonds, filberts, and hickories; butternuts, pecans, and black and English walnuts like a slightly acid or slightly alkaline soil.

The roots of nut trees are particularly susceptible to sun and wind, so try to keep roots moist until planting, and never let trees sit out in sun or wind. At planting time remove one third to one half of the top of the tree because in planting part of the roots are destroyed and cannot support the top growth at first. After the roots establish themselves, new growth will develop rapidly from the pruned branches.

Set trees in planting holes slightly deeper than they were at the nursery (you can usually see the soil line on the bark). Spread out the roots carefully, and put about 6 inches of soil in the hole; tamp down the soil with your foot. Now pour water into the hole to fill air pockets. Let the water seep into the soil, and then fill the rest of the hole with soil; pack down again and thoroughly soak again. If this sounds like a lot of water, it is, but it is necessary to ensure a good start for the young tree. Leave a slight saucerlike depression around the tree to catch rainwater.

Most nut trees come balled and burlapped, but some come bare-root (without protection) because it is cheaper to ship trees this way. Bare-root trees need to be planted as soon as possible after arrival. If you buy bare-root trees that are exceptionally dry, soak them with their entire length in water for several hours or overnight before planting.

Plant bare-root trees in well-dug holes, carefully spreading out roots. (If you see any damaged roots—cracked or broken—remove them before planting.) Fill in the hole with soil, making sure soil gets to the bottom of the hole and on all sides of the roots. (I do this with my hands, pushing down the soil carefully.) Then water soil thoroughly, let water soak in, add more soil to finish planting, and then again flood the soil.

A tree that has been transplanted goes through a shock, so the first year give the tree more than usual attention. Place a mulch of peat, straw, or even lawn clippings around the tree in a 3-foot diameter to keep roots cool in summer and conserve moisture. Be sure the tree has ample water; the soil should never become dried out, but do not drown the tree—keep soil evenly moist. You might also want to put some burlap or aluminum foil around the tree trunk to protect it from sun scald. The wrapping will eliminate sun scald, but I have never done it and my trees are fine. Still, it might be a wise precaution in areas with very severe hot weather. Also, remove the wire tags that are sometimes on trees because as the tree grows, the wire can split the bark and cause openings through which fungus can enter.

POLLINATION ·

The male flowers of nut trees appear in the form of a catkin that sheds its pollen in spring. The female flowers are at the end of a small nutlet that must open at the same time the pollen is available in order to be fertilized. On many trees the flower forms open at the same time, but if pollen sheds at the wrong time, other trees of the same kind must be close enough so wind can aid in pollination. Spring frosts can damage catkins, and sometimes trees will produce catkins for a few years before they produce nutlets.

INDIVIDUAL NUT TREES

ALMOND

This member of the rose family is a valuable and pretty tree, which is its problem: The white and pink blooms come out so early that they are very susceptible to frost injury—thus you get no harvest. The variety Nonpareil is the best one for California, but in northern states use Hall's Hardy, which blooms late and does not require cross-pollination. Almond trees will grow wherever peach trees will grow.

Plant almond trees in any well-drained location. Rich soil is not necessary; these trees grow well in even poor soils. Plant almond trees somewhat high because they settle a great deal after planting. In other words, do not dig the hole any deeper than necessary, and plant the trees with upper roots just below soil surface. Never plant the trees deeper than they grew in the nursery. Watch for sunburn on bark; wrap trees in burlap if sunburn occurs.

Fertilize almond trees only very lightly with a high nitrogen fertilizer, and if rains are regular, no additional watering is necessary (almond trees do not like wet feet). Prune lightly when you plant the tree, and prune again a little in summer.

Almond trees are not seriously bothered by pests and can fare for themselves without chemical intervention.

All almond trees require pollen from another variety for producing (honey bees are the pollinators).

CHESTNUT

The American chestnut tree is almost extinct, but the much smaller Chinese chestnut is available. This tree yields well. As with most early-blooming trees, the

Chinese chestnut should be grown on a northern slope to delay flowering so chill does not get the blooms. You will need to plant several trees, about 20 feet apart, to ensure pollination. Nuts generally appear in the fourth or fifth year, and from then on you should have high yields.

The chestnut tree is a beautiful, spreading, round-headed tree as cold-hardy as the peach and grows in a wide range of climates and soils. It will withstand −20° F. when fully dormant and lives a long time. The tree bears young and may even have a crop the second year after planting.

Grow chestnut trees in a rather sandy soil with plenty of organic matter. Unlike most nut trees, the chestnut needs buckets of water and excellent drainage. Pruning and care for the chestnut tree are about the same as for apple or peach trees. In other words, some work is involved here to get the trees to perform at their best.

The chestnut tree is rarely troubled by insects or disease.

Filbert and Hazelnut

The filbert and hazelnut trees bear a large crop. The filbert tree, which has the better of the two nuts, was imported from Europe, whereas the hazelnut tree is American—both nuts are similar in appearance and eating quality. Generally the filbert tree is used in areas of milder winters, the hazelnut tree for cross-pollination.

The best time to start your trees is in early spring. The filbert tree is good to grow because it needs no special requirements and does not have long taproots, so transplanting is easy. Filbert trees like a moderate nitrogen fertilizer. At planting time, prune the filbert tree 2 feet above the ground, leaving four to six branches. Prune very lightly thereafter until the tree is bearing.

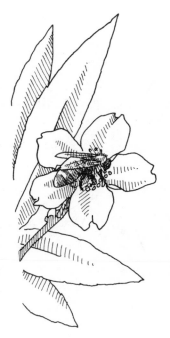

Use an eastern or northern location for the trees, and prune lightly every year, remembering to remove the root suckers. If you want a good yield of nuts, prune so that four or five main trunks carry the tree.

Filbert and hazelnut trees are rarely bothered by disease or insects.

HICKORY

Hickory trees are cousins of pecan trees. Common hickory trees are the shagbark, shellbark, and mockernut or pignut (the pignut is of little or no value). The hickory tree has an extremely long taproot, so it is a tough tree to transplant properly. The hole for the tree must be deep enough to accommodate a root of, say, 10 feet. Fill the hole gradually with soil, watering as you go along, and keep the area around the tree well weeded and mulched with fir bark, peanut hulls, or any organic matter that trees use for food.

Prune trees to avoid weak branches; you want a strong framework. Start the pruning when the tree is young.

Hickories are tough trees rarely bothered by insects or disease problems.

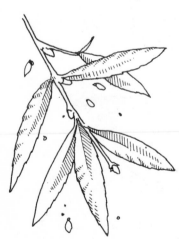

PEANUTS

Although the peanut plant is really a legume, it is so often thought of as a nut that it is included here. This is one nut crop you do not have to wait for, and peanuts will grow in almost any place where soil conditions permit. The three types of peanuts are Virginia, Spanish, and Runner; the Spanish type requires a light and sandy soil and warm climate.

The peanut flower has both male and female parts for reproduction and both parts are in the flower, so self-fertilization rather than the usual cross-pollination occurs. When fertilized, the ovary expands and forms a small weight that gravity carries to the soil. In the soil, the weight turns sideways, and a pod begins to form.

Plant peanuts 2 to 3 inches deep in rows spaced 24 inches apart. Pack soil down firmly around the seed. You can also plant shelled peanuts that way, but be careful not to break the papery covering of the nut.

After planting, peanuts need good warmth, moisture, and air. Seed germinates at about 70° F. In about one week roots will be growing, and lateral roots will form. At the same time, a white structure located just above the roots starts to enlarge. This structure pushes the halves of the seed coat upward. The emerging shoot cracks the soil surface in about one week. In another week leaves appear, and lateral branches start to develop; these branches are the origin of the flowering branches that develop later. Peanuts generally bear in about four months.

Soil must be evenly moist, neither too wet nor too dry, so a sandy loam is best for ideal growth. Harvest peanuts when leaves start to turn yellow and kernels are fully developed; skins will be light pink and papery thin. Harvest pods gently, so as not to pull up vines. Use a small digger or nimble fingers. Hang or stack peanuts loosely in a warm, well-ventilated area, or cure them about one week to ten days in air until the moisture content is right (about 10 per cent).

Store peanuts in dry, tightly covered containers. Refrigerate the containers because peanuts have lots of oil and can become rancid if left improperly stored.

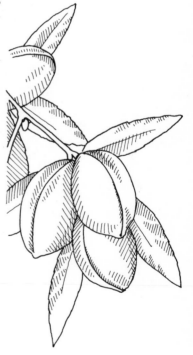

Pecan

The pecan tree is usually considered a southern tree that needs a long and hot growng season to yield its harvest. But some varieties can survive winters of −10° F. and still produce. Stuart and Schley are probably the most widely grown pecan varieties. Some pecan varieties mature late, others early, others are disease-resist-

ant, and still others are known for their ability to produce heavily. In other words, there is a pecan tree to suit everyone.

Unlike most nut trees, pecan trees do need a rich fertile soil and a readily draining area if they are to prosper. Plant trees in a deep, really deep, hole to accommodate the long taproots. Plant in early spring in the South, later farther north. Getting transplants to live through the summer is a tough job but not impossible.

Most varieties are self-fruiting, but sometimes catkins come in before nutlets or something goes wrong, so plant more than one variety. Also remember that wet weather during pollination time can severely reduce the distribution of pollen.

The major insects that attack pecan trees are pecan nut case-bearers, pecan weevils, and webworms. Apply the sprays for the pecan case-bearers in May; for pecan weevils, August or September. Contact your local agricultural agent for specifics since conditions vary in each part of the country.

To keep trees free of insects, use a dormant oil spray applied in late winter before leaf buds appear. This is when insects that hatch from eggs laid the previous fall are coming out. The insecticides mostly used for insects are Malathion and Sevin, which can be mixed with fungicides. The most serious disease of pecan trees is scab, a fungus that damages developing nuts and foliage in spring.

WALNUT

This favorite tree is a beauty, and for eating you will want the Carpathian, which is a cold-resistant, very hardy tree that yields lots of high-quality, thin-shelled nuts. Walnut trees need a very well-drained soil but not necessarily a rich soil. The true black walnut takes about one hundred years to bear, but the Carpathians usually yield six to seven years after planting, not that long when you consider the beauty and sweet taste of the walnut from the tree. (Recent reports indicate that black walnuts are toxic to other plants, like apples and tomatoes. The toxicity may be in the roots or leaves.)

The Carpathian or English hardy walnut is the tree most likely to succeed in most parts of the United States. It grows and produces well even in cold climates, and there are several varieties available, with perhaps Hansen and Merkel the favorites.

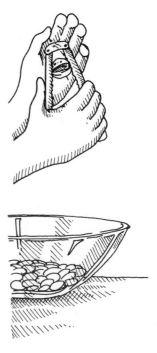

Plant trees in deep holes with adequate drainage and in good soil; walnut trees do not fare well in poor, gravelly soils. Most nut trees do not need extensive feeding, but the walnut does; a 10-10-5 fertilizer will be necessary to help trees bear. Feed trees about three times a year, and keep trees well watered because they do not like dryness at the roots.

Walnut trees do not like water around the trunk because they are susceptible to crown rot, a fungus that attacks the bark of the crown just below the soil line, so keep a 3- to 4-foot area around the tree without other plants that require watering. If you suspect crown rot, dig up soil around the trunk and expose the crown, letting the crown dry out. This usually arrests further infection. Or you can cut away rotted bark and apply Bordeaux mixture (at suppliers). My walnut trees have a base of large stones to prevent crown rot. The stones let air enter at the crown.

Walnut blight sometimes attacks trees, but this disease will destroy only the nuts, not the trees. Spray a fungicide early in the year, at the prepollen stage. Walnut aphids and caterpillars suck sap from the tree; control these insects with Malathion. Also use Malathion in repeated applications for walnut husk flies. Control scale by spraying trees with a dormant oil spray in February (follow the instructions on the bottle).

NUTS-AT-A-GLANCE

Nuts	Frost Damage	Soil	Life Span	Insect Damage	Cross-Pollination Needed	Remarks
Almond (Prunus amygdalus)	Occasionally	Neutral	Medium long	Usually not troubled	Yes	Grows well wherever peaches grow successfully
Chestnut (Castanea)						
Chinese (C. mollissima)	Very rarely	Acid	Medium long	Weevils	Yes	Seedlings preferred in North
Japanese (C. crenata)	Very rarely	Acid	Medium long	Weevils	Yes	Quality poor
Hazelnut or Filbert (Corylus)						
Filbert (C. avellana)	Occasionally	Neutral	Short	Filbert worm	Yes	Mites in some areas.
American (C. americana)	Rarely	Neutral	Short	—	Yes	Very hardy
Hickory (Carya)						
Shagbark (C. ovata)	Rarely	Neutral	Medium long	Usually not troublesome	Yes	Need extra care.
Shellbark (C. laciniosa)	Rarely	Neutral	Medium long	Some	Yes	Nuts thick-shelled.

Nuts	Frost Damage	Soil	Life Span	Insect Damage	Cross-Pollination Needed	Remarks
Pecan (C. pecan)	Rarely	Neutral	Long	Some	Some varieties	Need long growing season
Hybrids	Rarely	Neutral	Long	Some	Uncertain	Attractive trees
Peanut (Arachia Hypogaea)	Rarely	Neutral	Matures in 4 months	Leaf hoppers, soil pests	Yes	Needs long season of heat
Walnut (Juglans)						
Black (J. nigra)	Rarely	Neutral	Very long	Many pests	No	Differ in hardiness and pest resistance
Butternut (J. cinerea)	Very rarely	Neutral or slightly acid	Short	Fair	No	Very hardy
Japanese (J. sieboldiana)	Rarely	Neutral	Long	Fair	No	Fast-growing

9.
Berries

꙳ Most beginner gardeners overlook berries, and yet berries are an easy crop to grow and provide some luscious eating. And these members of the rose family have ornamental foliage that will add beauty to any garden. People tend to shy away from berries because they think the plants take up so much space. But this is not always true—berries can be tucked away against fences on trellises, above patios and on rafters, and so forth. They do not necessarily have to take over a garden if you plant them where you want them and keep them in bounds.

As with all plants, select the best varieties for your particular section. Blueberries are best in the cool northern section; use boysenberries in the humid South. You can grow strawberries in almost any part of the country.

GETTING BERRIES STARTED

Even if you do only half of what I am going to suggest, you will still have a good yield of berries because they are adjustable and easy plants to cultivate. Thoroughly prepare soil to ensure healthy and productive plants. Spade the ground, turn it, and add organic matter, usually compost. However, *never* add fresh manure to soil; manure for berries must be composted thoroughly and well rotted.

The soil for berries should be loose and have plenty of air spaces in it so drainage is excellent; berries simply do not like wet feet. To get berries started, dig a hole as wide as the width of a bushel basket and about 3 feet deep. Save the topsoil, but discard the subsoil if you can afford fresh soil. Throw some gravel and sand into the hole to provide the essential drainage facility. Now put the plant in place, add soil, and pack soil to the collar of the plant. Do not tamp down too hard on the soil—just firm the soil around the plant. Do not fertilize at first or you may kill the tender plants.

As with all plants, the sooner you can get berries into the ground the better chance they have of surviving the transplant. If you get your stock by mail order, soak the roots of your berry bushes (not strawberries) in a bucket of water for about two hours. Plant berries and vines as soon as possible, keeping roots away from direct sun and air.

Put stock in place 1 inch deeper than it was growing in the nursery. Make a small halo around the plant—a water well—and water copiously.

INDIVIDUAL BERRIES

BLACKBERRIES

Blackberries have long had the reputation of being a pest in the garden. That they certainly can be because they are invasive, but blackberries are also wonderful to eat as jams and jellies, so I can put up with them. (After all, if they get too rambling, you can always cut them.) Besides their take-over quality, blackberries have thorns, but now there are some thornless varieties available.

To keep blackberries from taking over, start growing them vertically on trellises. A well-grown blackberry plant can yield a lot of berries in a season, so you do not need too many plants to ensure good eating during the season. Like raspberries, blackberries have canes that will bear fruit the year after they sprout. When the canes die, new ones spring up to replace the old ones. An established patch can bear up to ten years.

In many ways blackberries grow like raspberries. But whereas raspberries are best for cool, moist regions, blackberries are best in milder climates and in the South. The blackberry is a shallow-rooted plant that requires ample moisture, good drainage, and protection from drying winds. Common blackberry varieties are hardy or semihardy or tender; pick the type that grows best for where you live. Plant in spring in the North and in fall or early winter in the South.

When plants arrive, trim away long roots and cut back canes to about 6 inches. Dig deep holes, spread out roots fanwise, and fill the hole with drainage material and soil. Pack soil rather tightly around the collar of the plant, and leave 3 to 5 feet between the plants, depending upon the variety.

There are bush- and vine-type blackberries. Bush

types need to be spaced 5 feet apart. When the new shoots that grow during summer are up to 36 inches, cut off the tips of stems to force growth of side branches. In the following spring, after flower buds appear, remove weak canes and thin others to stand about 10 inches apart. Now reduce side branches to 18 inches; the buds on the remainder of the side branches produce white flowers followed by fruit in midsummer. While the fruit is being produced, new growth is starting for another season's crop. Cut off the tips of these canes, and then late in the summer, after fruiting is over, cut away and destroy all canes that have borne fruit.

Vine blackberries need a slightly different pruning method. In the first season let the vines creep along the ground until they are 8 feet long, and then cut off the tips to encourage side branching. During summer, or early in spring, install supports (trellis or posts) at 10-foot intervals, and train canes on the supports. Cut back canes to 12 inches, and remove old canes after the season is over.

Harvest blackberries in midsummer when the berries are ripe and drop off at slight touch.

Bush-type berries can be propagated by digging up and replanting the suckers. Propagate vine types by tip layering; cover the tips with 2 inches of soil in midsummer.

Problems: Since blackberries are strong, vigorous plants, they are subject to few problems. Blackberry pests and diseases are likely to be the same as those for raspberries.

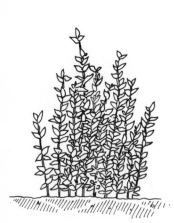

BLUEBERRIES

Blueberries like an acid soil, so if you do grow them, be sure the soil has a pH of about 4.2 to 5.0. To make your soil acid, add peat moss, partially decayed oak

leaves, or acid food. Do not add manure, which tends
to make soil alkaline.

Blueberries are largely self-sterile, so you will have to
have a few different varieties for plants to bear. There
are three good varieties: Highbush, Lowbush, and Rab-
bit-eye. The Highbush does well in North Carolina,
New Jersey, Massachusetts, and Michigan and grows
to about 8 feet. The Lowbush berry is a small plant, to
3 feet, and is fine for the New England states. Rabbit-
eye is best grown in the southeastern United States and
is a good plant because it adapts to many soil conditions.

Plant blueberries when they are dormant. This can
be in the spring or in the fall. Prepare soil carefully,
with sandy loam and perhaps some sulfur and sawdust.
Dig large holes for each plant, twice the size of the root
ball, and set plants 6 to 8 feet apart high in the ground,
with the crown 2 inches above the soil line. Feed plants
sparsely if at all because if fed too much, blueberries
will be all leaves and no fruit.

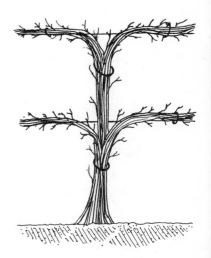

Do not fertilize when planting bushes; wait until
plants leaf out and are fully mature. When you transplant blueberries, cut back the plants to about halfway.
After planting, mulch plants with wood chips or sawdust.

Prune blueberry bushes in their dormant season in
winter or early spring. Remove weak growth and old
wood (largest fruit is borne on new canes). Cut back
tips of canes so only four or six flower buds are on each
twig or the plants will bloom themselves to death. Pick
off all blossoms the first two years, but allow a small
crop to mature in the third year. Then the crop will increase naturally year after year.

Blueberries cannot tolerate too much or even very little feeding because roots are so fine. Only fertilize if
plants indicate a deficiency (pale leaf color is one
sign). Then use a handful of cottonseed meal, which is
slow to release and non-burning.

Let fruits remain on the plant at least a week after they turn blue. To determine if berries are ripe for harvesting, twist them gently: They should fall off. Never pull or rip berries from the plant.

Problems: If grown properly, blueberries are incredibly free of insects and disease. Neglecting to pick fruit when it is ripe will encourage an entourage of fruit flies, so keep berries picked, and clean up all trimmings promptly. If insects do attack, dust plants with rotenone. Birds love blueberries as much as people do, so plant enough for everyone.

RASPBERRIES

Unlike strawberries, which produce only a few years, raspberries can produce as long as ten years. The types offered are red, black, purple, and yellow, in early, mid-season, and late varieties. Select types best adapted to your area of the country. Make every effort to secure one-year-old, virus-free plants.

Raspberries must have moisture to produce a really bumper crop; they also need excellent drainage. Plant red raspberries in early spring in northern sections, in fall in the South. Black raspberries are less hardy than red and more easily harmed by cold and thus should be planted in spring once weather is settled. Never allow plants to dry out completely or you will kill them.

Plant red or yellow raspberries 2 to 3 inches *deeper* than they were in the nursery, 3 feet apart in rows 8 feet apart. After planting, cut back red raspberries to 8 to 12 inches. (Do not plant black and purple raspberries as deeply as the red ones. Also, space them 6 feet apart, rather than the 3 feet for red raspberries.)

When the shoots of black or purple raspberries are 2 to 3 feet tall, start pruning the tips of new canes in mid-summer to encourage lateral branching that will bear the following year. By late summer or early fall, fruit buds develop; they will be dormant during winter. In spring, the laterals must be cut back to five or six fruit buds.

Let summer-fruiting red and yellow raspberries grow undisturbed until the second spring; when buds show green tips, remove all but three healthy canes per row of shoots to initiate lateral branches to bear fruit in mid-season. Cut back everbearing red and yellow types to the ground late in fall rather than in spring or early summer so they can grow during the summer to produce a heavy fall crop.

When they are fully ripe, pick berries every two or three days, preferably in late afternoon. Remember that berries are perishable, so do not jam them into gathering baskets; work judiciously. Once indoors, put berries in shade and coolness.

Red and yellow raspberries propagate themselves by runners under the soil. With black and red raspberries, tip-layer them by arching over the tips and covering them with 2 inches of soil; a new plant will pop up in spring. Cut off the tip, dig up the plant, and replant it elsewhere.

Problems: Raspberries have few pests or diseases. Buy mosaic- and leaf curl-resistant varieties. Red spiders may attack, but just hose them off. Eliminate white grubs with Malathion, and use rotenone dust to take care of any berry fruitworms.

STRAWBERRIES

Strawberries are an amenable crop that even the beginner can grow. These plants, which can be cultivated in most parts of the United States, are perennials that live for several years, blossom, and bear fruit each season. The best crops are produced the first two years; after that plants must be replaced. Strawberries are usually called everbearing, but they are really early, mid-season, and late bearers.

Even a dozen plants will yield a harvest for the novice, sparse in the first year but prolific in the second year. When you are ready to set your plants, trim back roots to 4 or 5 inches, dig holes wide enough to accommodate the roots, and set plants in place. Set plants so their crowns are at ground level. If crowns are too deep in the hole, growth will be retarded; if crowns are too high, plants will die. The plants need a rich moist soil and plenty of sun to do their best. The ideal soil is a sandy loam, but even in lesser soils strawberries prosper if there is good drainage. In the North, start the plants in spring; in the South, fall planting is fine. Just how you space your plants depends on how they are grown because there are several ways of growing strawberries (see below).

The strawberry plant, a member of the rose family, has lovely white scented blossoms that resemble wild roses. Plants grow close to the ground, with leaves produced on short woody stems. Most gardeners pinch the first blossoms from strawberries to get a better yield. This way the strength of the plant will not be depleted by setting fruit too early and the resultant crop when the plant matures will be heavy. I pinch off some, not all, of the blossoms and have a fine crop of berries. But not every strawberry flower produces fruit. Some blossoms do not have fruit, so cross-pollination is necessary (this is a natural thing done by insects or wind). Do not fertilize strawberries the first year; wait until the second year, when plants are mature.

There are so many ways to grow strawberries that it becomes a little confusing. Strawberry jars are fine if space is limited. Plants can also be grown in matted rows: Simply let mother plants set runners at will, until you have a solid bed of plants. Plants may also be grown in a hill system spaced 12 inches apart. Raised beds are still another way of having bushels of strawberries, and strawberry rings or pyramids can be accommodated in a 6-foot area.

Problems: The best way not to have insects or disease bother your strawberry plants is to select virus-free plants at the start. The most damaging insect is the strawberry weevil. This sucking insect can ruin a crop. The crown borer is another pest. Suitable preventatives are sold at nurseries. Verticillium wilt and gray mold are the two most prevalent diseases that attack the plants; these are carried by soil-borne fungi that infect the roots and kill the plant. Control for disease can be accomplished by using appropriate remedies (at nurseries). I cannot really recommend specific remedies or controls because I do not use them; my strawberries are rarely bothered by pests or diseases. Your plants will be healthy too if you grow virus-free varieties. *181925*

SPRAY SCHEDULE FOR BERRIES

Plant	When to Spray	Pest/Disease	Preventative
Blueberries	When blossoms have fallen; repeat twice at 7-day intervals	Flea beetles, fruit-worms, spittlebugs, botrytis rot	*Combination spray: Malathion, Carbaryl (Sevin)
Currants Gooseberries	Before growth starts in spring	San Jose scale, mites	Superior oil, 60- or 70-second viscosity
	When leaves have fully emerged	Aphids, leaf chewers, botrytis rot	*Combination spray as for blueberries
Raspberries Blackberries Loganberries	When leaves have fully emerged	Aphids, fruit worms, leaf chewers	*Combination spray (as for blueberries)
	Before blossoming		Same as for blueberries
	After blossoming	Aphids, leaf chewers, fruit-worms, cane borer	Same as for blueberries
Strawberries	When leaves have fully emerged	Aphids, leaf rollers, strawberry weevils, mites	Combination spray, (as for blueberries)
	Before blossoms appear	Same as above	Same as above

*Available ready mixed at suppliers.

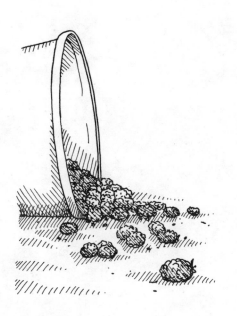

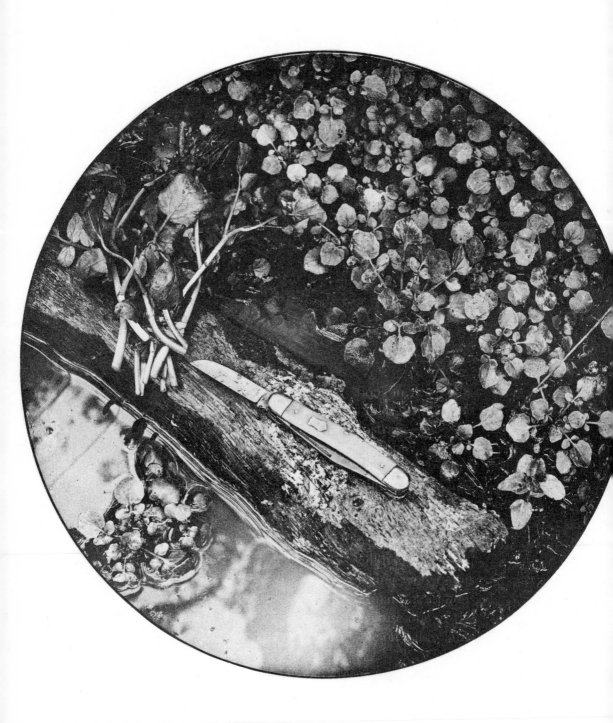

10.
Wild Plants

꒷ If you have followed the suggestions in this book, you will have plenty of fruit and vegetables for pleasure and profit. But even if you have gone astray—the yield is not great or good—you can still supplement the harvest with wild plants: blueberries and blackberries, for example; and, most importantly, wild greens. These greens have wonderful flavor and when properly prepared furnish beneficial nutrients as well as a new taste sensation. You can gather your own greens from the wilds, or perhaps some of the plants will be growing on your property. But remember that picking wild plants must be done with caution; there are many poisonous plants too. Know what you are picking; use one of the many good identification books available on wild plants in your area.

Let us look at some of the wild greens.

CLOVER

Red or white clover grows from 1 to 20 inches tall in meadows, pastures, open woods, and along roadsides. The foliage is three small, toothed leaflets. The young leaves and flowers are good when eaten raw, or dip them in boiling water for a few minutes to blanch them somewhat. Leaves can even be dried for winter use. If you like tea, try clover tea. Gather the full-grown flowers when they are dry. Then dry them indoors in the attic or a cool shady area for a few days. Now rub the flowers into small particles, and seal them in dry bottles. Use one teaspoon tea to each cup of boiling water.

DANDELIONS

Dandelions, which grow almost everywhere, are considered a pesky weed by most people, but they are also considered good eating by those who know a tasty, leafy treat. The tender young leaves are available in early spring—only the beginning leaves are excellent for eating. (Later, when plants blossom, the leaves become somewhat bitter.) Wash the leaves and eat them in a salad with a dollop of oil and vinegar, or cook them. To remove the leaves' tinge of bitterness, boil them in salted water. Then drain the leaves, and serve them with melted butter and a bit of lemon juice.

Dandelion roots are also good when cooked: Peel roots, slice them like carrots, and then boil them in salted water. Or, and this is an interesting variation on coffee, roast the roots slowly until they snap crisply when broken. Then grind the roots for use as coffee.

Dandelion wine is another treat. Pick one gallon of flowers without stems. Press the flowers into a large crock, and pour one gallon of boiling water over the flowers; let the mixture set for three or four days. Squeeze the liquid from the blossoms through cheese-cloth. To this brew add the juice of three lemons and one ounce of yeast. Cover the crock with a towel and let it sit for about 1 month while the mixture ferments. Then drain the liquid again and bottle the wine. Bottoms up!

DOCK

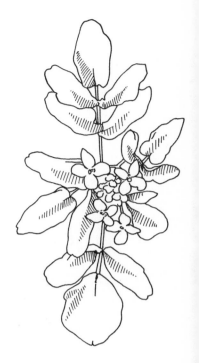

This wild edible has a slightly bitter flavor and grows abundantly throughout the United States. Sometimes known as wild spinach, dock is easy to find because the leaves have distinctive characteristics: They are 2 feet long, heart-shaped, and bright green. When picked young, dock makes a good salad vegetable, or rapidly boil it in a small amount of water until tender and then serve it with butter.

LAMB'S-QUARTERS

Sometimes called wild spinach, lamb's-quarters grows from 3 to 7 feet, with pale green leaves. You can usually find young plants to 12 inches coming up in spring; these are the tastiest. The leaves are excellent as a salad green, or lightly blanch them in water and eat them with oil and lemon juice.

MINERS LETTUCE

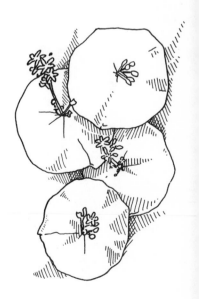

Miners lettuce has a pair of leaves growing together partway up the short stem; the leaves form a cup, with the stalk in the center. The stalk makes good salad eating when young and is a good substitute for spinach.

The leaves are succulent, differing in shape from the round leaves that encircle the tasty stems. Miners lettuce grows to about 1 foot tall in moist shaded areas in woods and gardens and occasionally along stream banks.

MOUNTAIN SORREL

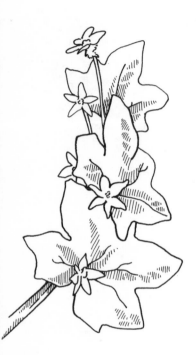

Mountain sorrel grows from a few inches to 2 feet from a large fleshy root. The leaves are small, one or two to a stem, smooth, and round or kidney-shaped. Freshly gathered leaves (before the plant blooms) are great for salads and potherbs. Prepare sorrel the same way as dandelion leaves for a delightful taste treat.

MUSTARD

Mustard is universally recognizable because of its brilliant yellow flowers, and it grows wild practically all over the United States. This annual plant, which grows to about 6 feet, is a relative of the cabbage, cauliflower, and similarly cultivated vegetables. Pick the fuzzy and somewhat hairy leaves when they are young. The leaves have a slight peppery taste when eaten raw. You can also boil mustard greens as you would spinach.

NETTLES

Nettles are difficult to gather (they are prickly, so you will need gloves), but they are not difficult to find. Nettles are vigorous plants that can grow to 7 feet. The leaves are coarsely veined, egg-shaped, and sharply toothed. Both stem and leaf have a fuzzy surface that contains irritating acids, but when dropped in boiling water the dark green nettles become tender and most eatable. Gather nettles in spring or early summer. Nettles are an excellent source of vitamins A and C and have a fine delicate flavor. Use nettles with butter and lemon juice for a good potherb.

PLANTAIN

Plantain is that familiar weed that grows even through city sidewalks. This wild plant has broadly elliptical green leaves that rise directly from the root about a straight central spike. Plantain leaves are rich in vitamins A and C. Wash leaves and eat them in a salad, or boil leaves for a few minutes in water.

PURSLANE

This is really an overlooked weed that grows practically everywhere and is excellent as a food source. The plant is a low grower, with jointed stems and purplish or green leaves tinged red. The narrow leaves grow to about 2 inches. Purslane's leaves are excellent salad greens once they are washed of grit. The simplest way to get leaves clean is to soak them in cold water in the sink. Then put leaves in salted boiling water and let them simmer for five minutes or so until tender.

Purslane is also a fine potherb when served with butter and lemon juice. If the somewhat slick quality of the plant bothers your taste buds, roll each young tip in flour, dip the tips in beaten egg and bread crumbs, and deep-fry the coated tips in hot fat for about seven minutes.

Tender young stems of purslane can also be pickled as a side delicacy.

ROSEROOT

This ubiquitous plant is able to grow in any soil and prosper. The fleshy leaves are pale green to yellow green, oblong to oval, and bear yellow flowers. To recognize roseroot, scrape the large thick roots: They have an aroma of rose perfume, hence their name. From summer to fall, the perennial roseroot can be used as a boiled vegetable or as a salad plant. Use only young leaves and roots because old leaves get bitter.

WATERCRESS

If you have never had watercress salad, you have certainly missed a good part of the good life. This succulent crispy green tops my list of salad edibles, and growing your own or picking it wild is lots of fun. Watercress has bright green rounded leaves on short stems and grows wild in cold streams and wet places over much of the United States. (It is quite expensive at the market.) Soak watercress in two Halazone tablets to one quart of water to make sure you get rid of any pollution aftereffects.

Do not confuse watercress with water hemlock (a poisonous plant); the latter grows taller. Positive identification of watercress is its three to nine segmented leaves, the biggest leaf at the base of the plant. You can use watercress for a salad or for a soup (quite fashionable in expensive restaurants), or even prepare a watercress sauce, which is good on chicken.

WILD CELERY

This plant grows in damp fields or beside moist road-sides from New England to British Columbia and Alaska. Gather wild celery in late spring or early summer, when it is still tender. The green stalks are hollow, with oil veins and often sticky patches. Plants grow to 4 feet, topped with clusters of flowers. The stems and leaf stalks should be gathered young; peel them and eat as you would celery. The stalks can also be eaten braised: First boil stalks for five minutes, and then braise them lightly in olive oil.

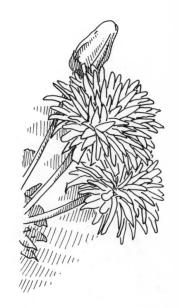

11.

Sprouts and Other Joys

SPROUTS

❧ Growing sprouts saves you money, and crisp green bean and mung sprouts will nourish your soul as well as your body. In salads or soups, or just as nibbles here or there during the day, sprouts are a refreshing treat and tonic. But what to sprout? For a starter, try alfalfa and mung beans, lentils and soybeans—these are sold at local health and organic food stores. Alfalfa sprouts, sometimes called the sprout of kings, are rich in minerals like potassium, phosphorus, calcium, and magnesium, and also in chlorophyll, and are good as a skin conditioner.

SPROUTING METHODS

Sprouts will sprout in (1) glass bottles, (2) flower pots, (3) cans, or (4) wood trays. Here are the "rules" for growing sprouts in each type of container.

Glass Bottles. Thoroughly wash and dry a mayonnaise jar. Stuff a handful of sphagnum moss (at nurseries) inside the jar, and add two ounces of beans and enough water to moisten the sphagnum thoroughly. Now drain the excess water. After draining the excess water, put a piece of cheesecloth on top of the jar and seal the jar with a ring cap (Mason jar type). You will be harvesting sprouts in a few days. This method is excellent for alfalfa and small amounts of beans.

Flower Pots. Use an 8-inch clay pot with drainage holes. Put a piece of burlap at the bottom of the pot, with a stone over it. Add two ounces of beans; cover the beans with a swatch of burlap. Use a stone to hold down this second layer of burlap. Add water; let excess water drain out. Cover the pot with a Baggie to ensure good humidity, and put the pot in a bright but not sunny place. This is a fine method for sprouting mung beans.

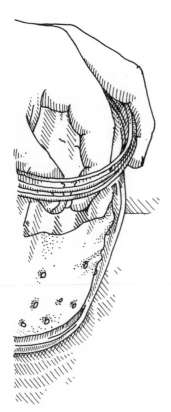

Cans. Cut out the top and bottom of a No. 1 can, and put a plastic cottage cheese or other carton into the can. (Be sure to punch drainage holes in the bottom of the container.) Place beans in the container, put a swatch of burlap over the beans, and weigh down the burlap with a small stone. Water the beans, let excess water drain out, and cover the whole can with a Baggie.

Wood Trays. Add a close-meshed wire screen to a nursery flat. Set beans on the mesh, cover the flat with cheesecloth, and water the beans. Then cover the flat with a Baggie.

RULES FOR GROWING SPROUTS OF ALL KINDS

1. To be sure there is air under the container, set the container on wood blocks or bricks.

2. Do not ever leave seeds in water for more than ten hours.

3. Use tepid water.

4. Do not sprout over four days or sprouts will become plants.

5. Do not ever let seeds or sprouts dry out. Water at least twice a day.

6. Do not buy treated seed; it may contain pesticides.

7. Do not put sprouts in sun; average bright light is best.

OTHER JOYS

WITLOOF CHICORY

Witloof (*Cichorium intybus*) is listed in catalogs as witloof or endive. A wild form, with blue flowers, is called chicory, blueweed, or coffeeweed, depending on which region you live in. Seed witloof in summer in the garden because it needs about 120 days to mature—get it planted and growing before the frost knocks it out. Witloof grows well in any sunny location in almost any soil.

You can harvest some of your witloof when you thin it in the summer. Thin plants when they are a few inches high, and use the tiny plants as a cooked vegetable—a good cooking green. Throughout the growing season you can take some leaves and use them in salads. (Do not use too many leaves because they have a slightly bitter taste; mixed with other greens, the leaves are fine.)

The expensive Belgian endive you see in stores is actually witloof root. Carefully dig out the whole witloof plant, including the root, in fall. Cut off all but a few inches of the leafy top. Plant the roots in a 16-inch-deep container that is 16×20 inches. Include drainage material and some charcoal in the container, and put in about 8 inches of soil, leaving 8 inches open at the top. Space the roots about 4 inches apart in the soil. If roots are too long, cut off the bottoms somewhat; roots should be 6 to 8 inches in length. Sink the roots level with the earth surface so that only the bit of stem you left on each root will show. Now fill the container with sand (or sawdust) to 1 inch of the top.

Keep the soil evenly moist and temperatures at about 40° to 45° F. In about a month sprouts should break the surface. This is your expensive Belgian endive. Cut the sprouts off at the base near the top of the root. The crop matures in winter. If you want endive all through the winter, plant in two or three sprouting containers at three-week intervals.

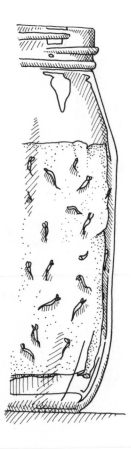

By the way, endive can be braised in butter and 1 teaspoon of beef stock for a fine cooked vegetable as well as its chief use as a salad green.

You can also make a coffee substitute from witloof roots. Use the witloof you grow to sprout endive. Peel the roots and dice or cut them into strips; put the strips on cookie sheets in the oven at 250° F. for about one hour, or until the plant is thoroughly dry and has a medium brown color. Then grind the chicory as needed for coffee.

All in all, witloof is a wise investment and I recommend it for every pleasure-profit garden. Here is one plant that gives cooking greens, luscious greens for salads, and a substitute for coffee. What more could you want?

MUSHROOMS

Today you can buy mushroom spawn in handy kits all ready for growing in a cool but not freezing cellar. Spawn is the root mass of the plant. There are two kinds of spawn: bottle spawn, produced in laboratories, and manure spawn, produced under natural conditions. There is really so little to growing mushrooms that instructions are almost superfluous. Keep the soil evenly moist, and harvest as instructed on the kit. The problem with kit mushrooms is that their flavor is not as good as those grown in soil, so if you are a perfectionist, plant mushrooms in soil. Mushrooms will thrive in almost any soil as long as it is kept moist at all times. Warm days and cool nights will produce a yield of mushrooms in a few weeks.

You can also grow mushrooms in mushroom flats or boxes; the boxes have already been filled with compost and "seeds." Treat these containers the same way as the kits to produce mushrooms. In either case, remember that if you have too many mushrooms, you can dry some.

Dry mushrooms on a sheet of hardware cloth in a warm draft of air, or place them on a cookie sheet in an oven at 130° F. with the door open for a few hours. Then soak the dry mushrooms in salted water before eating them (in case they harbor insects).

Because mushrooms are easy to grow by either method, in kits or in the ground, I suggest you have some of these plants on the property.

Sunflower Seeds

Sunflower seeds contain high amounts of phosphorus and calcium, which are essential to our diets. Since you eat sunflower seeds raw, nothing is lost in cooking. Also, sunflower seeds store well a long time without deteriorating.

The hearty sunflower plant (*Helianthus annuus*) is pretty in the garden, incredibly easy to grow, grows fast, and needs little help from you once planted. Harvest your sunflower seeds in the autumn, and dry them in a well-ventilated place or in the oven at low temper-

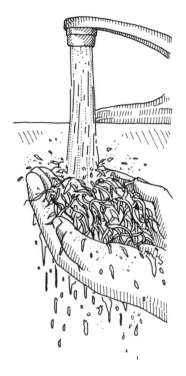

ature with the door open. Then store the seeds in dry glass bottles—you can have sunflower seeds for a year or more.

Pumpkin Seeds

Pumpkin seeds contain zinc, which is very important to the health of the entire reproductive system. Separate the seed from the pulp, and dry them as you would sunflower seeds.

Horse-radish

Most people cannot think of a good use for horse-radish, so they never grow it. Yet freshly ground horse-radish adds zest to any roast beef of boiled beef, as any Britisher will tell you. And of course horse-radish is an essential part of Jewish cooking and eating.

Horse-radish is really easy to grow and as a plant deserves the small space it requires in your outdoor garden. Plant it in early spring in a rich moist soil. Set pieces 2 inches long in the ground about 6 inches deep. Most gardeners plant in February and dig out the plants the following year because they spread rapidly, so you might want to contain them in tubs.

Watercress

Watercress was covered in Chapter 10 as a wild plant to pick; here we consider growing it as a cultivated crop. Watercress is easy to grow once it is established. A perennial plant, watercress continues growing year after year and is capable of being cropped continuously. If the conditions are right, you can harvest watercress for crispy salads and sandwiches year after year and at no cost. Repeated cuttings lead to repeated branching, and if the bed becomes crowded, just pull off shoots and thin out the crop. Watercress planted in spring will get growing readily and produce a good crop quickly; keep the plants closely cropped so they do not flower and go to seed.

There are two kinds of watercress—green and brown —but it is the brown *Nasturtium officinale* that is commonly cultivated. Watercress likes a limestone soil near clean, uncontaminated water, like a natural spring. Summer sun is not needed (only bright light); winter sun is fine.

The easiest way to grow watercress (but not the best) is to do it vegetatively. That is, pull up a crown from near a stream and start it on your property in a rich, very moist soil. You can also start tops by using the aerial portions of the plant, but getting watercress established this way is difficult. The thing to remember is that if you start watercress vegetatively, it is almost always subject to virus diseases. However, if you start plants from seed, the virus diseases should never be a problem.

To start watercress from seed, sow it in shallow containers of soil any time from April to August, and allow about eight weeks from sowing to maturity. Germination takes place in about ten days, and it is essential that the soil be kept evenly moist. Slightly mist plants with a hand sprayer every day until plants are growing well; then only a current or slow trickle of water at the roots is needed to bring watercress to perfection.

12.
Protecting the Bounty

❧ The specific chapters on fruits and vegetables, nut trees and so forth include information on insects and disease and how to eliminate them if they attack plants. This is a catch-all chapter about insects in general—mainly those you may not find in previous chapters—and what to do about them.

Proper cultivation of plants goes a long way in yielding healthy plants that are rarely troubled by insects and disease. Often it is cultivation, not insects or disease, that is the problem.

POOR CULTIVATION SYMPTOMS AND CURES

Plants develop brown leaves	Too much heat; fluctuating temperatures

New growth stunted	Not enough moisture
New leaves turn yellow	Soil pH may be amiss
Leaves with brown streaks	Sun scorch
Stems soft, leaves wilt	Too much shade; too much water

But even if your plant cultivation is good, if you have any kind of a sizable garden, you are going to have pests: insects, gophers, and other cute but destructive animals. And occasionally you may run into some plant disease problems. We covered these dilemmas in Chapters 5, 7 to 9 for vegetables and trees, but this over-all chapter will help you further to protect your bounty from invaders. Some precautions are necessary—do *not* let anyone tell you different! You can resort to chemicals to eliminate the problems, but in most cases you will then also eliminate most of the plants you want, so it is far wiser to battle the bugs intelligently, which means a quasi-organic method. However, this chapter is for *all* people, those who prefer to use chemical poisons and those who lean toward the safer preventatives, so it covers both organic and chemical prevention.

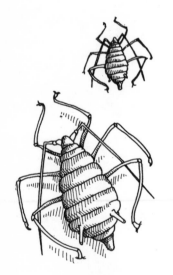

INSECT CONTROL METHODS

Before we present the chart of insects most likely to attack your plants, and what form of weapon you should use, let's briefly consider the several methods for fighting pests.

Spraying

With a spray you can reach all plant parts. Use a trombone-type sprayer, one that fits the garden hose, or a portable one. Before you spray, be sure the ground is moist, and spray in the early morning or late afternoon (do not spray in the middle of the day when the sun is at its zenith).

Dusting

This method is faster than spraying and eliminates the mixing process and the use of spray guns. Do the job on a calm day or your lungs will get more dust than the plants.

Spreading

This method involves spreading pesticide granules on the soil and then watering the soil thoroughly.

Systemic control

Systemics are granular or liquid poisons you sprinkle on the ground and water in. The poison is absorbed by plant roots, and all parts of the plant become toxic to many insects for about five weeks. Diasyston and Metasystox R are two systemics.

Biological control

This is by far the most intelligent way to eliminate bugs: fighting nature with nature. This method includes using ladybugs and praying mantises, good insects that eat bad insects; and natural preventatives like pyrethrum and rotenone, which are plant powders that repel insects.

INSECTS AND HOW TO CONTROL THEM CHEMICALLY

Insects	Appearance	What They Attack	Damage	Control
Aphids	Green, black, pink, yellow, or red soft-bodied insects	Almost all plants	Plants stunted, leaves deformed	Malathion, rotenone
Beetles (many kinds)	Brown or black, wingless	Flowers and vegetables	Eat leaves and flowers	Hand-pick, or use Sevin
Borers (many kinds)	Caterpillars, grubs	Woody and herbaceous plants	Wilting, holes in stems and branches	Diazinon
Caterpillars (including bag-worms, cutworms, cankerworms, tent caterpillars)	Easily recognized	All kinds of plants	Defoliate plants	rotenone, Diazinon, Malathion
Leafhoppers	Wedge-shaped insects that hop	Many plants	Pale or brown leaves, plants stunted	Malathion
Leaf miners (hollyleaf miners, boxwood miners)	Larvae of various insects	Many plants	Leaves spotted, blotched	Systemics, Diazinon
Mealybugs	White cottony insects	Many plants	Plants stunted, do not grow	Sevin, Diazinon
Scale	Tiny, hard, oval-shaped insects	Many plants	Yellowing or loss of leaves	Diazinon
Snails, slugs (not insects but common pests)	Easily recognized	Many plants	Eat foliage	Snare-all Cory's Snail Bait

PLANT DISEASES

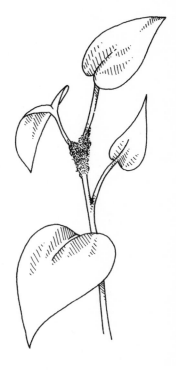

Many destructive plant diseases are caused by bacteria, fungi, and viruses. Bacteria cause blights, rot, galls, and wilts; fungi cause rot, wilt, rust, and powdery mildew; and viruses (often spread by aphids and leafhoppers) cause mosaic. Often unfavorable conditions and poor cultural practices open the way for these agents to cause trouble; a poorly grown plant, like a human being in poor health, is more susceptible to bacteria and viruses. Insects too can add to the disease problem because many of them spread diseases from one plant to another.

Environmental conditions are other factors in the development of bacterial and fungal attacks, especially excessive moisture and poor light. Moisture is particularly important because too much of it allows disease spores to germinate; excessive moisture in the soil can lead to root rot. Frequently, plants in shade are more prone to develop disease than those in light.

Disease Remedies

Following are some of the diseases that can occur in plants and the remedies. But quite frankly, once plants are infected, it is difficult to save them. Furthermore, highly poisonous controls are usually necessary. I list some of the chemicals here, but I sanction them *only* as a last resort.

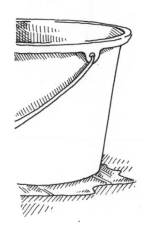

Rust. Leaves and stems have reddish spores in powdery pustules or gelatinous lumps. Foliage turns yellow. Several different kinds of rust affect hollyhock and snapdragon. *Control:* Spray with Actidione or Ferbam.

Powdery Mildew. White or gray growth, usually on the surface of leaves or branches or fruit. Leaves are

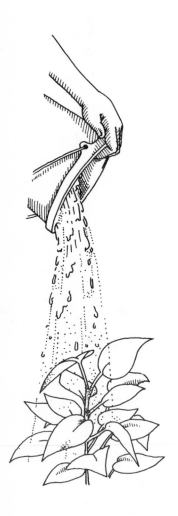

powdery, with blotches, and sometimes curled. Plants are often stunted. *Control:* Hose or heavy rain will naturally control powdery mildew.

Leaf Spot. Can do extensive damage to ornamental plants, resulting in defoliation. Leaves have distinct spots, with brownish or white centers and dark edges. Rarely fatal. *Control:* Spray with Zineb or Ferbam; cut off affected foliage.

Rot. Many different kinds of rot occur on plants. Affected spots look watery and turn yellow or brown. *Control:* Destroy infected plant parts. Sterilize soil before planting again.

Blight. Gray mold appears on plant parts. *Control:* For botrytis, spray with Zineb or Ferbam. For other blights, spray with Zineb, or treat soil with Terraclor.

Wilt. Can affect mature plants and seedlings. Usually wilt organisms live in soil. Cut away infected parts. *Control:* No known chemical control.

Mosaic. This virus disease causes a yellow and green mottling on leaves; leaves sometimes deformed. Plants are stunted. *Control:* Destroy infected plants.

Cankers. Lesions on woody stems, with fungi entering through broken tissue. *Control:* Cut away infected parts.

Dodder. A leafless, parasitic vine that suckers to the stem of the host plant. *Control:* Cut away dodder.

Galls. Enlargements of plant tissue due to fungi, bacteria, or insect attack. *Control:* Destroy plant.

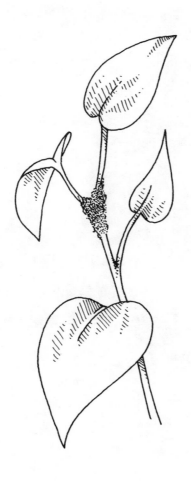

13.

Storage

The garden may produce lavishly in the summer, but come winter you can be without foodstuffs. However, you do not have to be because you can easily have some of the bounty—when properly stored—to use in the lean months.

The most common methods of storing vegetables and fruits are common storage, drying, canning, and freezing. (Common storage involves placing fruits and vegetables like apples and root vegetables in cool dark places such as unheated pantries, unheated but not freezing garages, cool cupboards, and so forth.)

Many people loathe the taste of dried vegetables and fruits, yet drying retains all vitamins but vitamin C, and the taste is quite acceptable once you get used to it. Just remember that the food must be stored in airtight containers in a cool dry place so spoilage organisms cannot grow. In some parts of the country there is enough sunshine to dry food naturally outdoors, but in most places it is better to use artificial heat.

Freezing, one of the simplest, easiest ways to preserve

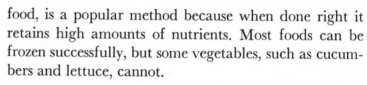

food, is a popular method because when done right it retains high amounts of nutrients. Most foods can be frozen successfully, but some vegetables, such as cucumbers and lettuce, cannot.

COMMON STORAGE

Many eastern homes contain root cellars, unheated areas with dirt floors where food can be kept cool but not freezing. Other storage places good to use are outdoor pits, barrels or boxes in the garage (bury the vegetables in sand in the barrels), or cellar rooms. The place depends on your climate and the facilities at hand.

Generally, common storage in one way or another works well for some varieties of apples, winter pears, and many vegetables: potatoes, carrots, beets, turnips, and squash. There are really no rigid rules to follow, only general ones because there are several methods of preparing the foodstuffs for storage. Here are some suggestions about common storage:

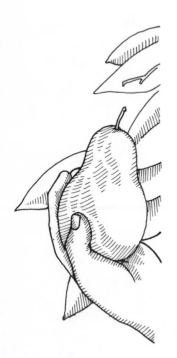

1. Handle the vegetables and fruits to be stored very carefully to avoid bruising them.

2. Let root crops cool a few hours after harvesting so the "field heat" can dissipate.

3. Dry vegetables before putting them into storage; this drying time varies with the vegetable, but usually a few hours to overnight is fine.

4. Keep storage temperature at about 35° F.

5. Be sure the storage area has good ventilation and humidity.

6. Leave some stems on foodstuffs when storing them.

7. Allow space between the foodstuffs in storage.

8. Be sure to keep the storage area clean.

CHART FOR COMMON STORAGE

Commodity	Place to Store	Temp.	Humidity	Storage Time
Vegetables				
Cabbage (late)	Pit, trench	32	Moist	Through late fall and winter
Carrots Beets	Pit, cellar	32	Moist	Through fall and winter
Cauliflower	Cellar	32	Moist	6 to 8 weeks
Onions	Any cool place	32	Dry	Through fall and winter
Parsnips	Cellar	32	Moist	Through fall and winter
Peppers	Unheated room	45-50	Moist	3 to 4 weeks
Potatoes	Pit, cellar	35-40	Moist	Through fall and winter
Squash	Cellar, basement	55	Dry	Through fall and winter
Tomatoes (green)	Cellar or basement	55-65	Dry	4 to 6 weeks
Fruits				
Apples	Cellar	32	Moist	Through fall and winter
Grapes	Cellar	32	Moist	1 to 2 months
Pears	Cellar	32	Moist	4 to 6 weeks

You can wash or not wash your food before storing it; I leave foodstuffs unwashed and have no problems. Just be sure the food is thoroughly dry before you store it. Use dry sand or sawdust as a packing medium.

If you do not have an indoor or outdoor area for common storage, build a cone-shaped mound outdoors in a well-drained location. Put a layer of bedding (straw or leaves) and then (to keep out rodents) a layer of hardware cloth on the ground. Stack the vege-

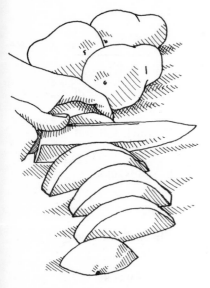

tables in layers on the cloth (do *not* store vegetables and fruits together). Now cover the pile with more leaves or straw, and over this put 3 to 4 inches of soil; firm the soil in place, and cover the soil with more straw and leaves. Put a board over the top of the soil to keep rain from entering. To be sure the mound is ventilated properly, place two or three stakes through the center of the pile, to form a flue. Cap the flue with hardware cloth (at hardware stores).

A pit—a wooden enclosure—works more or less on the same principle as the mound. The pit is generally 6 feet long, 3 feet wide, and 2 feet deep. Make a frame box to these dimensions; cover the sides with hardware cloth, and make a tight wooden lid for the top. Put a layer of sand in the box, layer in the produce, add another layer of sand, put in more produce, and so on. Now cover the top of the box with straw and plastic.

DRYING

Drying vegetables and fruits is probably the oldest method of preserving food. Fruit, berries, and root crops adapt well to drying techniques and can furnish a bounty of good food. Removing the moisture from the foodstuff reduces the possibility of bacteria or fungi growing (bacteria and fungi decompose foods).

Pick foods for drying promptly, when they are ripe, and dry them as soon as possible—a few hours is the rule. Use stainless steel knives for cutting to prevent discoloration of food, and cut the food into uniform slices or pieces. Onions and herbs need no precooking (blanching), but all other vegetables and fruits do, to inhibit enzymes within the food from growing. Blanching or preboiling is simple: First plunge the cut produce into boiling water for five to twenty minutes (see chart) and then into cold water for one minute, and then carefully dry the food.

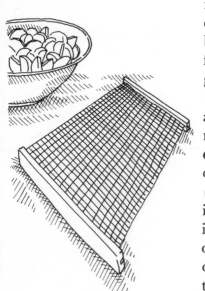

Sulfuring prevents discoloration, but I do not think it is really necessary. Steaming apricots and peaches, the foods most prone to discoloration, helps greatly to prevent discoloration. Merely place cut halves on pans or racks and steam the halves until the skins come off the flesh. Another way to avoid sulfuring is to immerse fruit in salt water for about twenty minutes, using one tablespoon of salt to one quart of water.

If you live in the right climate, outdoors put the food in single layers in trays or window screens; cover the trays with cheesecloth, to keep insects away. Set the trays in the hot sun, and stir the material several times during the day. Even in arid climates it will take all day to dry the food properly, in most climates at least two days. Pray it does not rain! Take trays in at night and put them out again the next day to avoid the rise in humidity that can ruin the drying process.

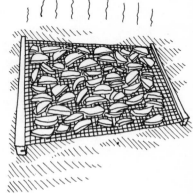

To dry food in your own oven, cover wooden-framed trays with coarse cloth. Preheat gas ovens to 150 degrees and leave the door open; be sure the flame does not go out. Move trays around to different levels so the food dries evenly: Move the top tray to the bottom, then to the middle, and so on. Set electric ovens at 200 degrees for the first few hours, and then lower the temperature to 150. Leave the door slightly open. The drying process will take about ten hours, so be prepared for a long haul.

The more you turn the food while it is drying, the better the product will be. Peach and apricot halves especially must be turned frequently during the drying process to provide an even distribution of heat. The food is dried when, after cutting through the food at the thickest part, you see that the texture and appearance are uniform throughout.

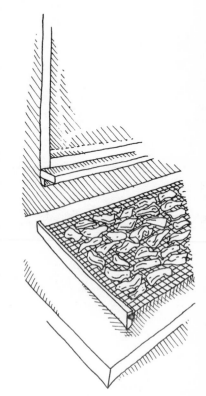

After drying, some people condition the food by putting the products in deep containers and occasionally stirring the food for about ten days. Then they reheat the food for about one hour at 150 degrees to prevent insect infestation. Then they store the food. This conditioning process may not really be necessary if you *immediately* store food in airtight containers in a cool dry place after drying the food. Glass jars with lids are fine as containers.

CANNING

Canned foods have an excellent taste and an appetizing appearance, and the jars are easy to store. But canning *must* be done correctly, with the proper equipment, or the food will spoil, which can literally spoil you. It is imperative that you heat fruits and vegetables thoroughly at the proper temperatures for the right length of time to eliminate completely organisms that might cause spoilage.

For canning you will need a canning kettle or pressure cooker, jar lifter, funnel and racks for cooling the jars, jars and lids, and measuring cups and spoons. Always use jars made for canning because old jars, those that once held commercially prepared products, may not tolerate high temperatures and may not have seal-proof lids. Regular canning jars may be reused, but *new* lids must be obtained each time to assure proper seal. Never use chipped or cracked jars of any kind for canning.

The two acceptable methods of canning foods are (1) pressure and (2) boiling-water bath. The pressure method processes food under pressure at a temperature of 240 degrees, to destroy bacteria that might spoil low-acid foods (most vegetables). This method is best for low-acid foods. The boiling-water bath method, which processes food at 212 degrees, is recommended for processing fruits, tomatoes, and pickles.

You will need a canning kettle (at hardware stores); the boiling-water method gives sufficient heat around jars of food in the canner to destroy organisms that

OVEN DRYING CHART

Commodity	Preparation	Cooking Time (Minutes)	Oven Temperature
Vegetables			
Beans (snap)	Wash, destem	20	150
Beets	Wash	Until done	150
Cabbage	Trim	12	140
Carrots	Wash, scrub	8-12	160
Onions	Skin	5-7	130
Peas	Shell, wash	3	140
Squash	Wash, stem, cut open, seed, and peel	15	150
Turnips	Wash, peel	7	150
Fruits			
Apples	Wash, peel, core	10	150
Apricots	Wash, halve, pit, and peel	10	140
Cherries (sour)	Pit and drain	12	130
Peaches	Wash, halve, pit, and peel	8	140
Pears	Wash, halve, pit, and peel	8	140

might cause spoilage in fruits and tomatoes. The steam pressure method is used for canning vegetables. *Never* use an ordinary pressure cooker pot designed for fast cooking.

Fruits may be packed hot or cold. To do cold packing (except tomatoes), fill jars with raw fruit and ladle hot syrup into jars to within ½ inch of the rim. To pack hot, boil the syrup and cook fruit briefly. Remove fruit from syrup and pack into jars; pour syrup over the fruit to fill jars to within ½ inch of rim. To make the syrup for fruits use two cups of sugar to four cups of water. Heat until sugar is dissolved. Don't let it boil away; keep hot.

The following schedule for water-bath canning is suitable for fruits (including tomatoes, which is a fruit) and pickles:

1. Prepare salt-vinegar water or sugar syrup (whichever is needed).

2. Fill water-bath canner half full of hot water and heat the water.

3. Wash jars and lids in hot soapy water, and then rinse them well.

4. Fill jars with food with boiling water or boiling hot syrup; leave one-third head space at the top of the jar. Wipe the top and threads of the jar before capping, and place each jar as it is filled on the rack in the canner.

5. Add boiling water to cover the jars in the canner 1 inch or so. Bring water back to boil.

6. When processing time is up, remove the jars with a jar lifter, and let them cool on rack.

Here is the schedule for pressure-canning vegetables:

1. Put about 3 inches of water into the canner, and then put the jars into the canner.

2. Place the canner over heat. Lock the cover, and leave the vent open until steam escapes for several minutes.

3. Close the petcock, and bring the pressure to 10 pounds. Cook foods as recommended in the following chart.

TIME CHART FOR CANNING KETTLE (WATER-BATH) METHOD

Fruit	Preparation	Pint (Minutes)	Quart (Minutes)
Apples	Wash, pare, core, cut up. Boil 3 to 5 minutes in syrup. Pack; add syrup; seal.	15	15
Berries (except strawberries)	Wash, remove stems. Add syrup. Seal.	10	10
Cherries	Wash, remove seed. Add syrup. Seal.	15	15
Pears	Wash, pare, remove core. Boil 3 to 4 minutes in syrup. Pack; add syrup.	15	20
Peaches	Wash, peel, pack. Add syrup. Seal.	15	20
Tomatoes	Scald 30 seconds; dip in cold water. Peel, core, cut in quarters. Pack. Cover with hot cooking liquid. Seal.	15	15

Note: The processing time given in this chart is for altitudes at sea level. For each 1,000 feet above sea level, add one minute to cooking time.

4. When the processing time is over, remove the canner from the heat, and let the canner stand until the pressure drops to zero. Wait a moment, and then open the petcock and tilt the cover away from you so steam escapes.

5. Remove the jars with a jar lifter from the canner. Stand them on rack to cool for about twelve hours.

6. Test for seal when the jars have cooled: Press the center of the lid; if the lid is in place properly, it will not move.

7. Label each jar with contents and date.

CANNING GUIDE FOR VEGETABLES
USING STEAM PRESSURE CANNING METHOD

Vegetable	Preparation	Processing Time (Minutes); 10 Pounds Pressure	
		Pint	Quart
Beans, green*	Snip or string; precook in boiling water for 4 minutes. Pack hot in jars, standing beans on end. Cover beans with boiling water or cooking liquid; leave 1/2 inch head space; seal.	25	30
Beets*	Scrub but do not peel; leave roots on and 1 inch of tops. Parboil until skins slip off. Peel, trim, and slice. Reheat. Pack hot into jars to 3/4 inch of top. Cover with boiling liquid. Seal.	35	40
Carrots*	Wash and peel. Cut in slices. Pack raw slices into jars up to shoulders to within 1 inch of top. Pour in boiling water to cover to 1 inch of tops. Seal.	30	30
Onions	Peel. Precook for 5 minutes in boiling water. Drain, save cooking liquid. Pack hot into jars to shoulders. Cover with cooking liquid. Leave 3/4 inch head space; seal.	25	25
Peas*	Shell. Hull and precook for 2 to 4 minutes. Pack hot into jars; leave 1 inch head room. Cover with boiling water to 1 inch of jar top. Seal.	40	45

Note: For altitudes higher than sea level, increase pressure 1 pound for first 1,000 feet in elevation and 1/2 pound for each additional 1,000 feet.

*Add 1/2 teaspoon of salt for pints, 1 teaspoon salt for quarts to jars before sealing.

All canned foods need proper storage in an area that is cool, dry, and well ventilated. Freezing will cause cracks in jars or may break a seal, allowing bacteria to enter the food. Properly processed foods should last about one year.

When you are canning you should know the signs of food spoilage, just in case. Gas bubbles, spurting liquid, bulging caps, any unnatural odor or color, cloudy liquid, or slimy food denote spoiled food that can be harmful to you. Throw it away! Never take chances with it.

Also, if you have not canned properly, there is a possibility that foods may contain toxins which will cause botulism poisoning. Botulism has no odor and is difficult to detect. The spores that cause botulism cannot grow in the presence of air and cannot thrive in acid foods. But the spores can grow and form a toxin in sealed jars of low-acid foods that have been *improperly processed*. Thus, as a safety factor it is a good idea to boil low-acid foods for about fifteen minutes to destroy any toxin that may be present if you made a processing error or if the pressure canner gauge was not accurate.

A very thorough booklet in canning can be obtained from the Ball Corporation, Muncie, Indiana 47302. (There is a small charge for the booklet.) The Kerr Glass Manufacturing Company, Sand Springs, Oklahoma 74063, also offers a home canning booklet; there is a small charge.

Helpful Hints on Canning

Do not process foods in mayonnaise jars or other jars prepared foods come in.

Use the boiling water-bath method for all fruits, tomatoes, and pickles.

Use the steam pressure method for all vegetables except pickles.

If you want to substitute a steam pressure canner for a water-bath canner leave the lid off the steam pressure canner and follow directions for water-bath canning without using the gauge or petcock.

Never reuse canning lids; seals must be perfect and used ones may be bent or impaired.

Ascorbic acid is an antibrowning agent and retards oxidation that browns food. It can be added to some fruits and vegetables.

It is best to can fruits with sugar syrup, but fruit juice, water, or honey may be used instead.

To cool foods always remove the jars from water they were processed in or the food will keep right on cooking as the water cools.

Always exhaust the pressure canner so air is forced out from inside the canner; otherwise temperature will not correlate with reading on gauge.

It is a good idea to heat home-canned low-acid foods (many vegetables) before you use them to boiling (210 to 215 degrees) for fifteen minutes to kill any spoilage organisms that may be present.

FREEZING

Drying and canning foods are popular ways of keeping surplus garden harvest. Another good way to preserve the bounty for future use is freezing, possibly the easiest method of all. Of course to do this you will need a freezer, but this piece of equipment, while initially expensive, pays for itself in time. Pick vegetables at the peak of maturity and freeze them immediately to ensure the greatest freshness.

To begin, wash vegetables thoroughly in cold water and blanch them; that is, cook them briefly in boiling water or steam. To blanch vegetables, use a large covered kettle and 1 gallon of water. Do no more than 2 pounds of vegetables at a time and place them in a wire basket (available at kitchen stores) or use a cheesecloth bag. Immerse the basket in rapidly boiling water for three to five minutes. Remove and immediately chill vegetables by plunging them into a kettle of icy water or simply holding them under cold running water.

Beans, beets, broccoli, carrots, peas, potatoes, squash, and peppers (do not blanch peppers) all freeze well. With greens such as spinach, reduce blanching to one to two minutes; same for peas. Tomatoes are not suitable for freezing.

It is important that the food to be stored is protected from the dry air of the freezer so proper packaging is perhaps the secret of good food freezing. You can package produce in plastic bags, heavy-duty aluminum foil, freezer paper, and so forth as long as the package will be airtight. When using plastic bags be sure to press out as much of the air as possible. Then seal. A new innovation in packaging is the heat-and-seal bag; Hamilton-Beach Sealobag is sold at stores. With this method the food can be frozen and reheated in boiling water all in the same bag.

Try to freeze produce in flat packages so they can be easily stacked. Keep freezer temperature at o° F. Do keep an inventory of what you freeze with dates and contents marked on the package.

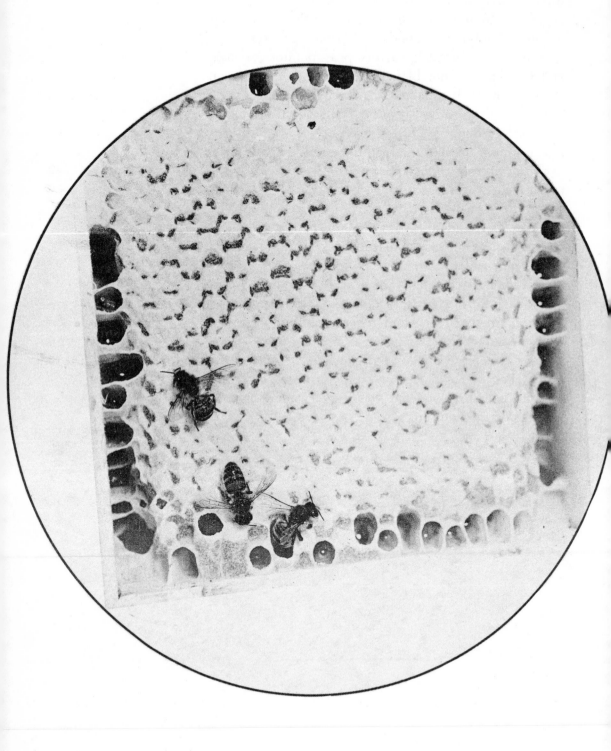

14.
Honey

Homemade honey is a taste treat that will please even the most hardened soul. And keeping a bee colony is not all that difficult because once you have the hives and the location, the bees do the work for you. Constructing the hives is the most work, but the actual time involved in keeping and tending the bees is minimal. Of course, collecting the honey is the best and easiest part!

GETTING STARTED

Start your own bee colony by buying an existing one from a local beekeeper or ordering the bees by mail (there are dozens of suppliers). Do *not* try to collect wild bees because they are vicious and you will end up with stings, not honey. The breed of the bees is an important consideration to true bee enthusiasts, but for

you, who just want honey, Caucasian or Italian breeds are fine.

THE BEEHIVE

The beehive is the bees' home, and the modern hives are convenience in themselves, quite unlike the old straw types. The combs can be easily removed without harming the bees. A hive is simply a series of boxes to hold frames. On the frames, bees put down combs; they fill the combs with honey. When the frames are filled, remove them. The hive is constructed so that many frames can be added to the series. Expanding the hive cuts down on swarming, which is good because if a hive gets too crowded, the workers are liable to produce another queen, and you might lose half your colony to the new queen.

A basic beehive kit (from suppliers) includes a standard hive, comb foundation, and frames. You will also need gloves and a bee veil, a feeder, a smoker, and hive tools.

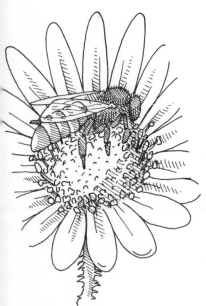

Once you put the hive together (instruction sheets come with the package), fill the frame with comb foundations. Bees can of course build their own combs, but in *their* own way, in an unevenly surfaced design. You should prepare the combs in *level* sheets in each individual frame so you can get the most honey out of the least space.

The comb foundation is essentially a sheet of finished beeswax combs. Thus part of the comb is already built for the bees; the bees will complete the job for you. In other words, if the combs are already there, the bees will make honey, not combs—bees make cells only when they need them.

Some people make comb honey, but you want extracted honey. Making comb honey involves keeping the queen isolated in the bottom of the hive, which can be a tricky procedure. To make extracted honey, all you have to do is work with two chambers. The top chamber is empty. When the bottom chamber is full of hatching eggs, place it on top, moving the empty chamber to the bottom. The queen bee, who lurks underneath the bottom chamber, keeps on laying eggs: All she sees above her is an empty chamber, not realizing that you have removed the chamber with the eggs.

EQUIPMENT

Get a bee veil first—this is a must—and use leather or canvas gloves up to the elbows. Smoke applied in the right quantities subdues bees (but does not overwhelm them), so get a bee smoker. You direct the smoke to where you aim it while you gather the honey. Also get a hive tool, a steel strip curved at one end, to pry off covers, remove frames, and scrape off residue gum deposited by bees in unwanted places.

Commercially sold bees come in 2- or 5-pound wire cages. The queen bee comes packaged separately in her own cage. Spring is the best time to start your colony because the fruit trees are blossoming and there will be enough pollen for the brood.

Decide where you want the hive before the bees arrive (if you buy them). The best location is a bright one because intense sunlight can harm bees. Also, you want the apiary near nectar-producing plants, but do not put the hives under trees or the hives will not get enough sun. Wind can wreck beehives, so select a protected place, a site that has a good circulation of air but no severe winds; an area against a fence, sheltered by trees, or near a hedge is a good place for a hive.

The entrance of the beehive should be away from frequently traveled paths because bees coming home from a supply run instinctively zero in on the hive—anyone, like you, in their way might be stung.

STARTING THE HONEY FARM

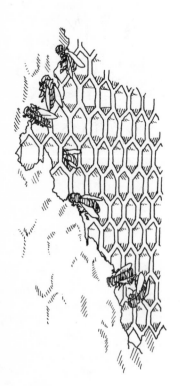

When your bees arrive, put the cages in a cool shady place and let the bees get settled for a few hours. In the meantime, mix a solution of two parts sugar to one part water. Coat the cages with the syrup so the bees can have their fill. Leave the bees in the cages all day so they can get as much of the sugar solution as necessary; move the bees at dusk into the hive (they are more apt to settle down at dusk anyway). Take the cover off the hive. To get the bees into the hive, tip the bee cage slightly over the hive, putting a piece of cardboard or canvas over the cage so the bees will migrate downward and not upward and out. (The bees must get down to the comb foundations prepared for them.) Slide the bees out slowly while lowering the cage. Then take the queen cage out of the bigger cage. At one end of the queen's cage is a perforated door; remove this door to expose the "candy" used as the actual door. The bees will nibble away the door to get to the queen. Put the queen's cage between the middle frames and just below the one holding the shipping cage. Invert the shipping cage over the spot where the queen is suspended.

You will have to supply the initial honey, so refill the feeder can with more sugar and water solution. Cover the shipping cage and the feeder can with canvas draping down so the bees cannot remain in the empty shipping cage. On the second day, take out the shipping cage but leave the canvas and check to see that the hive entrance is open. A boardman feeder (from suppliers) on which you have placed an inverted Mason jar should be put at the bee entrance and used to feed syrup.

In about a week, when the weather is pleasantly warm during the day, check to see if the queen is laying. You will know the queen bee by her swollen belly and the many workers tending to her. The cells around her will be both capped and uncapped; the uncapped ones should have little white eggs. If these eggs are present, everything is working right. At the end of the first week, remove the syrup can, canvas, and empty shipping cage, and retop the hive with its inner and outer cover.

HINTS ON BEEKEEPING

1. Always choose a warm day to work on hives because bees are less temperamental in good weather.

2. If it has rained, wait a day or so before working with bees.

3. When you are ready to invade the hive, have the bee smoker at hand.

4. Be sure you are wearing the proper clothing and arms, legs, and hands are covered.

5. When you lift the top cover, do it slowly. Use the hive tool to lift the inner cover a fraction of an inch so you can get some smoke in there. Puff in smoke gently, and then puff in some more smoke to drive the bees down between the frames. Now lift off the cover entirely.

6. Keep smoking the bees down as you inspect the hives.

7. Lift the frame gently by both ends. The cover will be swarming with bees, so be careful not to mash them.

8. Close the hive slowly.

15.
Your Own Wine

⚠ Whether for your palate or for the eye, grapes, once established, do their thing without much help. But do not think of opening a winery; you can get some homemade wine for the table out of the deal, but not enough for hundreds of bottles.

GRAPES AND HOW TO GROW THEM

European grapes are cultivated in California, but American varieties will probably thrive anywhere in the country. From the family *Vitis, V. labrusca* is an eastern variety—the Concord is an example. *V. rotundifolia* is a southern grape—this includes the wonderful scuppernong and muscadines—and *V. vinifera* is our western grape.

Most people shy away from grapes because they have

read something about the complex job of pruning and training. But for our purposes grape growing can be made simple. Unless there are grapes already on your property, you will be starting fresh, which is usually the best way. Buy one-year-old stock from local suppliers, who will have the type that grows in your area. The one-year-old vine with a good root system is easier to establish than, say, the two-year-old transplant. When selecting grapes, look for a bushy and solid root system, the key to a healthy plant.

In vineyards grapes are usually grown on a southern hill, where they gets lots of sun and good air circulation. For home growing, you can actually start grapes in any area that has *some* sun (at least five hours a day) and good air circulation (but not gales). Remember that grapes are vining plants and so will need some support. You do not have to install supports the first year, but by the second year grapes must have a trellis or arbor to climb. Use twine to tie your vines loosely and firmly to the support.

Plant grapes in a well-drained fertile soil; dig up the soil and crumble it with a rake and hoe, and use a lot of humus to get the plants growing well. (The soil should be mixed and ready for the vines when you get them.) Grapes grow best in a neutral soil, one with a pH of 6 or 7. Space grape plants about 8 feet apart, always keeping in mind that once grapes start growing, they really grow and take up more space than you think. In other words, do not overplant grapes.

Some initial pruning will be necessary to encourage the important development of feeder roots. Vines have a double set of roots, one set aboveground, the other set, which spreads out, belowground. The feeder roots are the roots aboveground. To prune the vine, cut back all canes but two. Leave two or three buds on each cane. Spread out the roots on a layer of topsoil in a large hole 24 inches in diameter and at least 24 inches deep. Fill in the hole with soil so the new plant sits a little lower in the ground than it did in the original container. Make a saucer around the plant to facilitate watering. Water the soil thoroughly and deeply.

Once plants are growing, keep them well watered so they are heavy and thriving. The rooted vines should be heavy and well grown—water does the trick. Keep the ground around the vines level and well tilled; that is, soil should be broken up, not caked. Break up soil gingerly with a rake so as not to injure roots. If the soil is very poor, apply a 5-10-5 fertilizer before spring to help plants along. Grapes do not have stringent requirements, but they will need your help if they are in very poor soil, so tend them regularly as you would other plants.

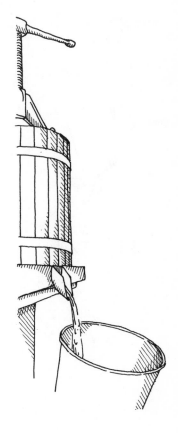

Do not get involved in the hundreds of different ways to prune grape vines. Just remember that in the second winter pruning is really important, to shape the plant. Prune in the late winter, after the leafy growth has come out, and leave a little more wood than the previous year. Leave about ten buds on each of the main canes. Cut off all laterals but one from each cane; these remaining laterals become the main canes in the following year. The laterals must be kept growing horizontally (on the support), so training is absolutely necessary. In spring the new growth can be trained to grow vertically.

If well grown, grapes can thwart most insects, although a common disease problem is a fungus called black rot. The grapes rot from the inside out; if you see this, immediately remove the grapes so the disease does not spread. Chemicals will not help this disease—you can only minimize this disease, not really cure it. Thrips may occasionally attack grapes, but they can be eliminated with a commercial spray. If the grape berry moth invades your grapes, consult your local agricultural department for necessary remedies.

Grapes are ready for harvest when stems begin to dry slightly. Harvest your grapes in the morning. Use scis-

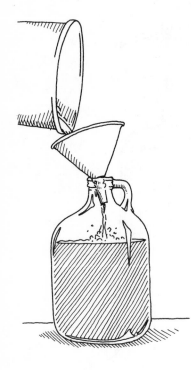

sors, and do not twist the stems. Set the grapes in a cool shady place.

All grape plants take at least three years to bear, so do not expect an immediate vinery.

WINE MAKING

Wine making involves picking the grapes, crushing and fermenting them, and bottling the product. And yes, drinking too! Your homemade wines may not measure up to the superior quality of the commercial ones, but they will be quite enjoyable and not watery. Homemade wines will not be filtered, so your wine will have a robust quality lacking in most other wines.

You will need a saccharimeter (sugar tester) (from suppliers) and a plastic jar to test your grapes. Squeeze and strain the grape juice into the jar, filling the jar with enough juice so the sugar tester can be floated in the juice. The tester has degrees marked on it, like a thermometer, so you can measure the density or sugar content of the juice. This is necessary because the alcohol content in the finished wine will be about half that of the sugar content. For a good wine you will need at least 18 to 26 degrees of sugar as measured on the tester; 21 to 23 degrees will make a balanced wine of 11 to 12 per cent alcohol.

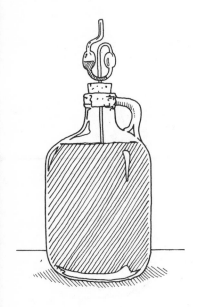

After you have tested the crop for sugar content, crush the grapes—hand-squeeze rather than trying the foot crushing played up in the movies. Fill a 'liquid-tight vat, barrel, or a plastic tub with the juice. Because the juice will ferment, fill the container only three fourths full, to leave space for the fermentation process.

You can ferment the wine by leaving it alone—the yeast in the air will start the fermentation—but generally you need a yeast starter. Buy wine yeast from suppliers, putting it in the container at the same time you are putting in the crushed juice. The fermentation may take several days or several weeks, depending on the weather: The cooler it is, the longer fermentation takes. Usually the juice will lose all its sugar in about ten days. When the bubbles stop, fermentation is nearly done. Use the sugar tester occasionally to see how things are progressing. (Since you have crushed the whole grape, you will have stems, skins, and seeds to get rid of. These solids boil to the top and should be removed as soon as the juice is done or taken off the first few days.)

When the sugar content of the juice has reached zero, pour the pure juice into a wine barrel. (Large glass jars are dangerous because the last remaining bubbles can build up enough head to crack the glass.) Make a fermentation bung (siphon) for the barrel: a bent tube coming from the barrel into a glass of water. The bung will let the last gases escape from the pure juice into the water without letting air into the juice.

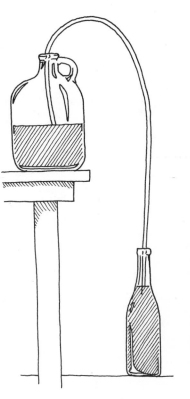

A siphon can be elaborate or simple. All you really need is 1 yard or so of clear plastic tubing, but this is rather hard to manipulate and may dip down and suck up some of the deposit. So buy a siphon tube from a wine dealer. Put the fermentation jar or barrel on a table and an empty fermentation jar on the floor. Insert the siphon tube into the wine on the table; keep the tube off the bottom, where the sediment is. Now lower the other end of the tube to a point lower than the bottom of the wine; place the siphon tube in your mouth and suck. When the wine is flowing in the tube, put the tube into the neck of the lower, empty jar. Let the wine flow until it moves into the neck of the bottle on the floor. When the wine reaches one third the way up the neck of the jar, pinch the tube slightly but firmly to stop the flow. Do not do this suddenly or the flow may churn up some of the deposit in the jar on the table. If you happen to stop the flow of the juice in the siphon, just suck the end of the tube to get it running again.

STORING WINE

Chemical actions and interactions occur during the maturing process. Esters are formed, and the strengthening of the wine's flavor and bouquet is taking place. The wine needs oxygen for these desirable changes to take place. Oxygen percolates through the bung to the wine in about six months to mature the process. After six months, slice the bung level with the top of the jar, and cover the surface of the cork and jar rim with sealing wax to get an airtight seal. Try to cork the wine bottles as soon as possible so the wines are not exposed to air too long—you do not want the possibility of spoilage organisms. Be sure to cork the wine bottle securely. Use dark-colored glass bottles for your wine; light striking light-colored bottles causes wine to lose its color. Wine that has lost its color will leave a flat taste on the palate. Store your wines in a cool, dark, waterproof cellar or similar area for at least six months, to mature.

16.

Share the Bounty

The idea of urban gardening and farming on empty city land is gaining momentum, and rightly so. It offers many pluses: (1) improves the appearance of a neighborhood by utilizing land that may have become litter-strewn; (2) gives people a sense of community spirit and group effort (badly needed these days); (3) offers children a chance to participate in gardening; and (4) provides fresh vegetables at little cost.

How to get the soil ready, the seed growing, and the plants in the ground are of little concern. There is not too much cost involved; work is necessary, but once people know about the garden, they will participate for part of the bounty. And a local newspaper ad will be good publicity for the community garden. What is not usually so easy is securing permission to use open land for vegetable gardens; getting permission involves reaching the right people. But newspapers will help make your plea known, and your local city representatives and city hall can be contacted to get things started.

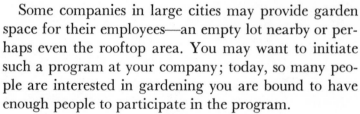

Some companies in large cities may provide garden space for their employees—an empty lot nearby or perhaps even the rooftop area. You may want to initiate such a program at your company; today, so many people are interested in gardening you are bound to have enough people to participate in the program.

Also check with local botanical gardens; many times they have a gardening program for children and have already acquired a plot of land that can be used in community gardening.

STARTING A COMMUNITY GARDEN

After you secure permission from planning authorities, private citizens, church groups, or other sources to use the land for a garden, select one person to spearhead the drive and coordinate materials and time. You will need someone willing to devote some time to getting it all together. Once the land and leader are selected, divide the land into equal plots, with one plot to each family or group, or the entire garden can be shared by a group of people. It is far better for each family to have its own garden than for many people to try and cultivate a large area together.

The first step is to clean the land of debris by the hand-and-rake method—hard work but worth it. Next, have the land turned over. Rototilling is the easiest and best method; rototilling gets the land ready fast for growing and saves time and muscle work. (See the yellow pages for earth-moving companies.)

When the land is tilled, order some good topsoil. This is expensive, but if you want a good yield of vegetables, you will need fresh, nutritional topsoil. A 6-yard truckload of topsoil generally costs about $65, and for the average 25×100 plot, two truckloads can do the job. Spade and mix the topsoil into the ground and break up all soil so you have a bed that is porous and well turned.

Planting the garden will be little problem; it is fun to get the seeds or prestarted plants in the ground, so everyone will be willing to participate. Sow seed as described in the vegetable chapter (Chapter 5), and refer to that chapter for when and how to plant. Once seeds are in the ground (and remember to leave ample space between rows for walking and tending plants), you must be sure that the seeds or seedlings get even moisture. This is the hard part because for the first few weeks constant watering is almost essential to get things growing. Select members of the group to water on specific days, say, one person for Monday and Wednesday, another person to do it Friday and Sunday. In other words, keep an almost round-the-clock schedule for watering the first two weeks.

KEEPING IT GOING

Start picking weeds the minute you see them so they do not sap the soil of nutrients that the vegetables need. I do not believe in weed killers, so I suggest you hand-pick. If this is done twice a week, hand picking is not that gruesome and provides good exercise. Again, select certain people to weed and thin on designated days, and have all phone numbers posted on a call sheet in case someone gets sick or cannot tend to the garden on a particular day. Then he or she can call and get a substitute.

Thin, weed, and water plants through harvesttime, and once a week have everyone assemble to see how things are going and growing. The more team spirit, the better the garden. And once the first radishes and carrots are harvested, there will be little problem in finding participants to help in the next garden planting.

Harvest the vegetables when they are ready, dividing the harvest as equally as possible so everyone gets his full share (do not forget to let the kids get into the act too).

In my zest to get you started in community gardening I have neglected to mention the insect-prevention details. Have a knowledgeable person, one who has had some experience in gardening, protect the community garden plants against insects and diseases. This individual must be one who realizes the full importance of keeping the land clean of pests; without proper pest control, the entire garden could be wiped out. (Refer to Chapter 12 for full details on how to cope with the insects.)

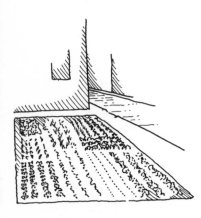

WHERE TO LOOK FOR FREE LAND

Here are some suggestions for getting the land for these gardens:

1. Look to *schools,* which may contribute some land to the program.

2. Ask *large companies* with landholdings if they would contribute some land (they might, for good public relations).

3. Seek out *church groups;* many churches own vacant land.

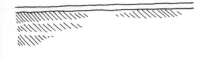

4. Run small inexpensive *ads* in *local papers* asking for privately owned land to use for vegetable growing.

5. Ask local politicians/*county officials;* they may have access to land areas that can be used for community farming.

6. Consult your *local planning office* and ask for land for vegetable growing.

7. Get your project known by newspapers or any other *media.*

17.
Help for Free

⤜ No matter what garden problem you have, and no matter how hopeless it seems, there is free and expert information to help you combat the problem—if you know where to find it. Whether you are fighting an aphid infestation on your favorite crop or rust on the fruit trees, there are government agencies—the United States Department of Agriculture (USDA), Agricultural Extension Services, and the United States Forestry Service—to help you help your plants.

There is also help for your plants at your local nursery. However, I have found through the years that you must select the *right* nursery, with *qualified* people who can answer your gardening questions, because in many places help and advice are transient. Most owners of small nurseries are well-qualified people who know the plants of their district—what will and will not grow. These are valuable people to go to, and invariably they will take the time to answer your questions. Indeed, they will often volunteer information when you buy.

VARIOUS GOVERNMENT SERVICES

The various government services lead the list of useful suppliers of information about everything from *Agave* to *Zantedeschia*. This bounty of knowledge is at your fingertips: a phone call or a postage stamp away. Do not expect quick replies or catered humbleness from these services, but if you are reasonably patient you will have your questions answered, and free or minimum-cost pamphlets about specific subjects will be sent on request.

As with all bureaucracy, there are levels of authority. Do not give up before you start. Often if you start within your own state, you will not have to go any further. Some of the government agricultural services are listed in your local phone book under County Agency, County Extension Service and Soil Conservation Service, and so on. (For USDA, look under the United States Government listings in your local phone book.) If these people cannot help you, they will tell you who can. Be explicit, have definite questions, and do not bother these services unduly. Remember, they are generally understaffed and extremely busy. However, also remember that you are paying their salaries, so learn how to use them to your benefit. Working within the system does have its benefits if you know how to do it. If you have insect problems in your garden, do not run to your local nursery and buy endless remedies. They are not necessary and they cost money. Call your county agent and explain the situation. He will try to identify the insect if you send it and tell you what to do to combat it. If your trees are dying for no reason, go to the phone again; call the county agent and ask him if some blight or insect has invaded the area. He will advise you just how to proceed.

In addition to your county and state helpers there is the federal government, the largest source of published

gardening information. The address for their list of publications (45 cents) is: United States Department of Agriculture, Superintendent of Documents, U. S. Government Printing Office, Washington, D.C. 20250. The USDA offers pamphlets, booklets, and hardcover books dealing with plant diseases, seeds, trees—an array of gardening subjects. The pamphlets are clear, concise, and reasonably priced: 20, 35, and 40 cents. (The definitive books about special subjects cost $3 or more. This material may be heavy reading and not full of glorified pictures, but within these books is solid information written by experts in the field.)

Some large cities (for example, New York, San Francisco, and Chicago) have central offices for the federal government publications. You can buy their booklets and books covering various aspects of gardening and land, thereby eliminating the letter writing and postage costs. These city offices and their addresses are:

Government Printing Office
710 North Capitol St.
Washington, D.C. 20402

The Pentagon
Main Concourse
South End
Washington, D.C. 20310

Department of Commerce
Lobby
14th and Constitution Ave. NW
Washington, D.C. 20230

USIA Building, 1st Floor
1776 Pennsylvania Ave. NW
Washington, D.C. 20547

Department of State
Building, 1st Floor
2201 C St. NW
Washington, D.C. 20520

Room 1C46
Federal Building, U.S.
Courthouse
1100 Commerce St.
Dallas, Texas 75202

Room 1421
Federal Building, U.S.
Courthouse
1961 Stout St.
Denver, Colorado 80202

Room 135, Federal Office Building
601 East 12th St.
Kansas City, Missouri 64106

Room 100, Federal Building
275 Peachtree St. NE
Atlanta, Georgia 30303

Room G25, JFK Federal Building
Sudbury Street
Boston, Massachusetts 92203

Room 1463, 14th Floor
Everett M. Dirksen Building
219 South Dearborn St.
Chicago, Illinois 60604

Room 1015
Federal Office Building
300 North Los Angeles St.
Los Angeles, California 90012

Room 110
Federal Office Building
26 Federal Plaza
New York, New York 10007

Room 1023, Federal Office Building
450 Golden Gate Avenue
San Francisco, California 94102

The United States government, as mentioned, supplies a list of all their publications for 45 cents. From this master list you select the price list (and titles) of gardening subjects that interest you.

> National Parks
> Insects
> Forestry
> Plants
> Soils and Fertilizers
> Ecology

In addition to the above subject booklets, new subject listings are issued about twice a month. The twice-monthly listings (called *Selected U. S. Government Publications*), about popular and new subjects, are free on request. Write for this selected list to: Public Documents Distribution Center, Pueblo, Colorado 81009.

From the 45-cent price list, here are some pamphlets available. Most are priced from 10 to 25 cents. To order, write to the Superintendent of Documents, U. S. Government Printing Office, Washington, D.C. 20250. Supplies are limited and prices are subject to change without notice.

> Home Planting by Design, 1969
> Home Propagation of Ornamental Trees and Shrubs, 1962
> Suburban and Farm Vegetable Gardens, 1969
> Plant Hardiness Zone Map, 1965
> Pruning Ornamental Shrubs and Vines, 1969
> Pruning Shade Trees and Repairing Their Injuries, 1965
> Selecting Fertilizers for Lawns and Gardens, 1971
> Aphids on Leafy Vegetables
> Controlling Disease of Raspberries and Blackberries
> Dwarf Fruit Trees, Selection and Care
> Growing Black Walnuts for Home Use

Growing Blackberries
Growing Cauliflower and Broccoli
Growing Nectarines
Growing Vegetables in the Home Garden
Strawberry Varieties in the United States

In addition to the above fine publications, there is also a list of yearbooks from the USDA that is worth its weight in gold; the list includes:

Seeds, Yearbook of Agriculture, 1961 ($3.50)
Plant Diseases, Yearbook of Agriculture, 1953 ($3.50)
Landscape for Living, Yearbook of Agriculture, 1972 ($3.50)

On request from the local government printing office in your city (listed previously) or from Superintendent of Documents, U. S. Government Printing Office, Washington, D.C. 20250, you can receive the list of yearbooks free.

Another publication of the United States Government Printing Office is a special *Home Garden Brochure,* which you should have. This is available from the Public Documents Distribution Service Center, 5801 Tabor Ave., Philadelphia, Pennsylvania 19120, and offers a variety of pamphlets about gardening. Following is a brief résumé: Prices vary from 10 to 30 cents. Supplies are limited and prices are subject to change without notice.

Growing Vegetables in the Home Garden
Growing Tomatoes in the Home Garden
Ants in the Home Garden and How to Control Them
Mulches for Your Garden
Minigardens for Vegetables

New brochures on various garden subjects are issued throughout the year so check with the above address.

As you can see from the above list, there are helpful booklets about almost every garden subject. Although the booklets are not definitive (some are only eight pages long), there is enough valid information to get you started in the right direction. Prices, you will note, are certainly low for the amount of information given.

Order well ahead of time because supply is limited and publications are sent by fourth-class book rate mail, which takes several weeks.

Thus, even with a very minimum expenditure, you the gardener can accumulate a very good, inexpensive garden library to help you help your plants. Once you have some knowledge of the gardening scene and about specific plants—trees, shrubs, vegetables—you can purchase regular garden books. In other words, you will have some idea of what you want, and will spend your money wisely.

For the most part we have concentrated on gardening on a small scale, but the United States government also offers publications for those interested in commercial gardening and farming, such as setting up an orchard, running a small farm, and so on. Upon written request and receipt of nominal charge, the USDA will also supply you with maps of your area. These maps indicate yearly rainfall, first frosts, and other pertinent weather information. They can help you greatly in determining your weather growing conditions, especially if you are new in the area. Remember, the plants you grow are more or less governed by climate, which includes rainfall and temperature. These maps can save you needless worry in determining the kinds of plants for your garden.

OTHER PUBLICATIONS

Before we leave free or minimal-cost pamphlets, brochures, and books, I want to mention the fine publications offered by the Brooklyn Botanic Garden. These handbooks are reasonably priced and offer solid information about various gardening subjects. They are not the final answer, but they certainly are an excellent start to get you gardening.

These horticultural handbooks range from 64 to 112 pages, are prepared by experts, and can be ordered by name or number from Brooklyn Botanic Garden, 1000 Washington Avenue, Brooklyn, New York 11225. Here is a brief list of some of their booklets (all cost $1):

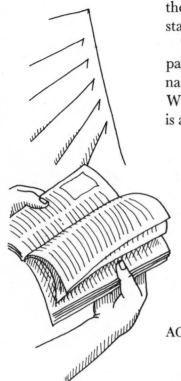

⁑20 Soils
⁑21 Lawns
⁑25 100 Finest Trees and Shrubs
⁑26 Gardening in Containers
⁑34 Biological Control of Plant Pests
⁑49 Creative Ideas in Garden Design

AGRICULTURAL EXTENSION SERVICES

As a taxpayer, your Extension Service is your private answering advisory tool. Questions about raising plants, pest fighting, and soil can be answered here. Address letters (and be specific about questions) to the following locations:

Agricultural Information
Auburn University
Auburn, Alabama 36830

Agricultural Information
University of Alaska
College, Alaska 99701

Agricultural Information
College of Agriculture
University of Arizona
Tucson, Arizona 85721

Agricultural Information
University of Arkansas
P. O. Box 391
Little Rock, Arkansas 72203

Agricultural Information
Agricultural Ext. Service
2200 University Avenue
Berkeley, California 94720

Agricultural Information
Colorado State University
Fort Collins, Colorado 80521

Agricultural Information
College of Agriculture
University of Connecticut
Storrs, Connecticut 06268

Agricultural Information
College of Agricultural Sciences
University of Delaware
Newark, Delaware 19711

Agricultural Information
University of Florida
217 Rolfs Hall
Gainesville, Florida 32601

Agricultural Information
College of Agriculture
University of Georgia
Athens, Georgia 30602

Agricultural Information
University of Hawaii
2500 Dole Street
Honolulu, Hawaii 96822

Agricultural Information
College of Agriculture
University of Idaho
Moscow, Idaho 83843

Agricultural Information
College of Agriculture
University of Illinois
Urbana, Illinois 61801

Agricultural Information
Agricultural Administration Building
Purdue University
Lafayette, Indiana 47907

Agricultural Information
Iowa State University
Ames, Iowa 50010

Agricultural Information
Kansas State University
Manhattan, Kansas 66502

Agricultural Information
College of Agriculture
University of Kentucky
Lexington, Kentucky 40506

Agricultural Information
Louisiana State University
Knapp Hall, University Station
Baton Rouge, Louisiana 70803

Agricultural Information
Dept. of Public Information
University of Maine
Orono, Maine 04473

Agricultural Information
University of Maryland
Agricultural Division
College Park, Maryland 20742

Agricultural Information
Stockbridge Hall
University of Massachusetts
Amherst, Massachusetts 01002

Agricultural Information
Dept. of Information Services
109 Agricultural Hall
East Lansing, Michigan 48823

Department of Information
Institute of Agriculture
University of Minnesota
St. Paul, Minnesota 55101

Agricultural Information
Mississippi State University
State College, Mississippi 39762

Agricultural Information
1-98 Agricultural Building
University of Missouri
Columbia, Missouri 65201

Office of Information
Montana State University
Bozeman, Montana 59715

Department of Information
College of Agriculture
University of Nebraska
Lincoln, Nebraska 68503

Agricultural Communications Service
University of Nevada
Reno, Nevada 89507

Agricultural Information
Schofield Hall
University of New Hampshire
    Durham, New Hampshire 03824

Agricultural Information
College of Agriculture
Rutgers, The State University
New Brunswick, New Jersey 08903

Agricultural Information
Drawer 3A1
New Mexico State University
Las Cruces, New Mexico 88001

Agricultural Information
State College of Agriculture
Cornell University
Ithaca, New York 13850

Agricultural Information
North Carolina State University
State College Station
Raleigh, North Carolina 27607

Agricultural Information
North Dakota State University
State University Station
Fargo, North Dakota 58102

Cooperative Extension Service
The Ohio State University
2120 Fyffe Road
Columbus, Ohio 43210

Agricultural Information
Oklahoma State University
Stillwater, Oklahoma 74074

Agricultural Information
206 Waldo Hall
Oregon State University
Corvallis, Oregon 97331

Agricultural Information
The Pennsylvania State University
Room 1, Armsby Building
University Park, Pennsylvania 1680

Cooperative Ext. Service
University of Puerto Rico
Mayaguez Campus
P. O. Box AR
Río Piedras, Puerto Rico 00928

Agricultural Information
University of Rhode Island
16 Woodwall Hall
Kingston, Rhode Island 02881

Agricultural Information
Clemson University
Clemson, South Carolina 29631

Agricultural Information
South Dakota State University
University Station
Brookings, South Dakota 57006

Agricultural Information
University of Tennessee

P. O. Box 1071
Knoxville, Tennessee 37901

Department of Agricultural Information
Services Building
Texas A&M University
College Station, Texas 77843

Agricultural Information
Utah State University
Logan, Utah 84321

Agricultural Information
University of Vermont
Burlington, Vermont 05401

Agricultural Information
Virginia Polytechnic Institute
Blacksburg, Virginia 24061

Agricultural Information
115 Wilson
Washington State University
Pullman, Washington 99163

Agricultural Information
Evansdale Campus
Appalachian Center
West Virginia University
Morgantown, West Virginia 26506

Agricultural Information
University of Wisconsin
Madison, Wisconsin 53706

Agricultural Information
University of Wyoming
P. O. Box 3354
Laramie, Wyoming 82070

Information Services
Federal Ext. Service
U. S. Department of Agriculture
Washington, D.C. 20250

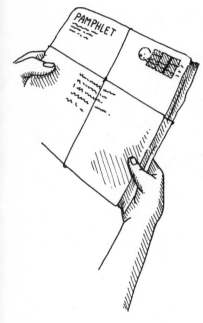

CONSERVATION ORGANIZATIONS

These organizations are mainly concerned with keeping the ecology intact, which is no easy chore these days. Although protection and conservation are the organizations' main goals, the groups are also generally well schooled in soil and plant problems. One segment of nature governs another, and membership in these conservation groups will keep you abreast of the latest legislation about conservation, ecology, and related matters. By all means, if you have any questions about ecology or conservation, write and ask questions. Make yourself heard.

The American Forestry Association
919 17th Street, NW
Washington, D.C. 20006

Friends of the Earth
30 East 42nd Street
New York, New York 10017

The Izaak Walton League of America
1326 Waukegon Road
Glenview, Illinois 60025

National Audubon Society
1130 Fifth Avenue
New York, New York 10028

National Parks and Conservation Society
1701 18th Street, NW
Washington, D.C. 20009

The National Wildlife Federation
1412 16th Street, NW
Washington, D.C. 20006

The Nature Conservancy
Suite 800, 1800 North Kent Street
Arlington, Virginia 22209

Sierra Club
1050 Mills Tower
San Francisco, California 94104

The Wilderness Society
729 15th Street, NW
Washington, D.C. 20005

MAIL ORDER SEED COMPANIES

Burgess Seed & Plant Co. P. O. Box 218 Galesburg, Michigan 49052	Seeds and plants
W. Atlee Burpee Co. Philadelphia, Pennsylvania 19132 Clinton, Iowa 52732 Riverside, California 92502	Vegetable and flower seeds, fruits, ornamentals
Farmer Seed and Nursery Co. Faribault, Minnesota 55021	Vegetable and flower seeds, fruits, ornamentals
Earl Ferris Nursery Hampton, Iowa 50441	Fruits, berries, ornamentals
Gurney Seed & Nursery Co. 1448 Page St. Yankton, South Dakota 57078	Vegetable and flower seeds, fruits, berries, ornamentals
Joseph Harris Co. Moreton Farm Rochester, New York 14624	Vegetable and flower seeds
Kelly Bros. Nurseries, Inc. Dansville, New York 14437	Vegetable and flower seeds, fruits, berries, ornamentals

Earl May Seed & Nursery Co. 6032 Elm St. Shenandoah, Iowa 51601	Vegetable and flower seeds, fruits, berries, ornamentals
Nichols Garden Nursery 1190 North Pacific Hwy. Albany, Oregon 97321	Vegetable seeds
L. L. Olds Seed Co. 2901 Packers Ave. Box 1069 Madison, Wisconsin 53701	Vegetable and flower seeds
Geo. W. Park Seed Co., Inc. Greenwood, South Carolina 29646	Vegetable and flower seeds
Clyde Robin P. O. Box 2855 Castro Valley, California 94546	Herbs, wildflowers, vegetables
Stark Bros. Nurseries Louisiana, Mississippi 63353	Fruits and ornamentals
Stokes Seeds Box 548 Main Post Office Buffalo, New York 14240	Vegetable and flower seeds

Catalogs are available from most suppliers; some are free; most carry a minimum charge.

Index

Index